ROUTLEDGE LIBRARY EDITIONS
MARXISM

Volume 4

JAMESON, ALTHUSSER, MARX

JAMESON, ALTHUSSER, MARX
An Introduction to *The Political Unconscious*

WILLIAM C. DOWLING

Routledge
Taylor & Francis Group

LONDON AND NEW YORK

First published in 1984

This edition first published in 2015
by Routledge
2 Park Square, Milton Park, Abingdon, Oxon OX14 4RN

and by Routledge
711 Third Avenue, New York, NY 10017

Routledge is an imprint of the Taylor & Francis Group, an informa business

© 1984 William C. Dowling

British Library Cataloguing in Publication Data
A catalogue record for this book is available from the British Library

ISBN: 978-1-138-85502-1 (Set)
ISBN: 978-1-315-71284-0 (Set) (ebk)
ISBN: 978-1-138-90060-8 (Volume 4) (hbk)
ISBN: 978-1-138-90062-2 (Volume 4) (pbk)

Publisher's Note
The publisher has gone to great lengths to ensure the quality of this reprint but points out that some imperfections in the original copies may be apparent.

Disclaimer
The publisher has made every effort to trace copyright holders and would welcome correspondence from those they have been unable to trace.

JAMESON, ALTHUSSER, MARX

AN INTRODUCTION TO
The Political Unconscious

William C. Dowling

Methuen

First published in Great Britain
as a University Paperback in 1984 by
Methuen & Co. Ltd
11 New Fetter Lane, London EC4P 4EE

Printed in Great Britain by
J. W. Arrowsmith Ltd, Bristol

British Library Cataloguing in Publication Data
Dowling, William C.
    Jameson, Althusser, Marx: an introduction to
    The political unconscious.—(University paperback 871)
    1. Jameson, Fredric. Political unconscious
    2. Criticism   3. Hermeneutics
    4. Narration (Rhetoric)   5. Communism and
    literature   6. Fiction—History and criticism
    I. Title
    801'.953   PN81.J29

ISBN 0-416-38410-2

Contents

Preface

What follows is, unabashedly, an introduction to Fredric Jameson's *The Political Unconscious*. It is not a study, not a critique, not a survey of contemporary Marxist criticism or Jameson's place in it, but simply an attempt to make the very demanding argument of one seminally important book available to readers who have heard about its importance but have so far been baffled by it. In recent years, as there has been an explosion in theory and tremendous pressure from the convergence of a number of modern disciplines, such introductions have become necessary and common, but the custom so far has been to reserve them for writers who are either deceased or European (or both). So perhaps I may say a word about why Jameson, as a living American theorist, needs an introduction.

He does not, in one sense, need an introduction at all: among those who follow contemporary theory Jameson has already established himself as the most important Marxist critic now writing, and *The Political Unconscious* carries his enterprise to a new level. Indeed, the book could claim a seminal importance on either of two separate grounds: as the first

9

sustained attempt to extend into cultural studies in English the Marxist renewal originating in the work of Louis Althusser in France, and as an original and powerful attempt to subsume within an expanded Marxism the rival programs of such thinkers as Jacques Derrida, Michel Foucault, and Gilles Deleuze. We are, as I've said, in the midst of an explosion in theory, and a number of younger theorists especially show signs of rapid development, but so far Jameson is the only one working in English who writes as the peer of the French poststructuralists. Purely in the toastmaster's sense, then, his work needs no introduction.

The Political Unconscious needs an introduction, in short, not because of its undoubted importance but because it is difficult. As anyone can testify who has tried to read the book without help, or who has followed the articles Jameson has been publishing in the interval since his earlier *Prison House of Language* and *Marxism and Form*, his thought has in recent years steadily grown knottier and more complex, his manner of presenting it more oblique and compressed. Putting aside for the moment the reasons why Jameson is in no sense guilty of a merely perverse opacity, I may remark at the outset that the difficulty is less than it seems. With the relevant background in contemporary theory and contemporary Marxism filled in, and with Jameson's own central concepts somewhat expanded, his book becomes entirely readable. That is the main reason for providing an introduction like this one.

Still, the mere fact of Jameson's difficulty, or of a writer in English needing an introduction in plainer English, is likely to infuriate the people who remain in high dudgeon about the obscurities of such writers as Derrida and Lacan. Why, to ask the question that always gets asked about such writers, can't he just come out and say what he means? I must confess to a certain sense of weariness when I encounter this question now, one doubtless dating from the time a few years ago when I was trying to master *Grammatology* and never could manage to explain to various intelligent and genuinely interested friends "what this Derrida is saying." What Derrida was saying, I later realized, was that you can come right out and say what you mean only if you've got a false theory of meaning, but even so, he never *said* that directly, and . . . (These are the frustrations one felt.)

The problem raised by *Grammatology* and *The Political Unconscious* alike, that is, is the problem of style as enactment: a way of writing that *shows* as well as *tells* what it is trying to get across. Thus Derrida cannot just "come out and say what he means" because the whole ethic of coming out and saying what you mean is based on the referential notion of language whose essential and monumental falsity Derrida is trying to expose. In the sunlit world of Anglo-American empiricism, you and I (our minds, at least) are over here, and the world is over there, and language is the expendable or disposable means of saying what we want to say about it. It has been the business of Derrida and those writing in English under the sign of poststructuralism to suggest that both that world and its attendant style, the plain style enjoined by the Royal Society in the late seventeenth century, may add up to nothing more than a comfortable illusion—that, on the contrary, language may have created the world, and that there is a certain inescapable treachery in the way it did and does so.

For Jameson, on the other hand, the question of style as enactment is the Marxist question of theory and praxis. In his view, the plain style is the limpid style of bourgeois ideology where there is no need for obscurity because all truths are known in advance (except the central and terrible truth that can never be acknowledged, that this pleasant world of known truths is rooted in exploitation and oppression and domination). A genuinely Marxist style, then, will be one that produces what Jameson calls (in *Marxism and Form*) a sense of "dialectical shock," that as the price of its intelligibility again and again forces the reader out of customary and comfortable positions and into painful confrontations with unsuspected truths. As Jameson also says, a dialectical style is one that makes you hear the shifting of the world's gears as you read.

There is, Doctor Johnson remarked, more of pain than of pleasure in the progress the mind makes through any book. He was thinking, in the eighteenth-century way, not about novels or mystery stories but about what we would now call intellectual prose. What Jameson means by dialectical shock does include *that* sort of pain, the pain we have all felt of trying to follow a difficult argument, but it implies another sort of pain as well, the pain of seeing history, as a committed Marxist must, as a nightmare from which the only escape lies in political and social revolution. This too is the price of reading Jameson with genuine understanding. (A question may arise whether an introduction like the present one does not destroy the effect. The answer, of course, is yes: dialectical shock is, as Robert Frost said of poetry, what is lost in translation. But the reader who comes to *The Political Unconscious* through this introduction may then go on to experience Jameson's more difficult argument as it stands.)

Jameson is difficult for other reasons as well; they may be briefly stated. One is the host of embarrassments that in contemporary Marxism goes under the name of "the problem of Stalin" (or "really existing socialism")—Marxism as historically embodied in various actual governments has not turned out very well, and Marxist philosophy as such has no good explanation why. That is, there hangs over Jameson's head as a Marxist critic the accusation that, as the *nouveaux philosophes* like to say, Marxist social theory is a machine for constructing concentration camps, and the current embarrassments of Poland and Afghanistan, as well as the memory of Stalin's Gulag, press hard upon his argument. The practical effect of this is that Marxist critics must always be situating themselves in relation not only to non-Marxist readers but also to various theoretical positions within Marxism, so that crucial parts of the argument are written in a kind of code. This too is a source of obscurity that I try to resolve in the following chapters.

Another reason for Jameson's difficulty is that, as I have intimated, he is trying to neutralize the entire program of contemporary poststructuralism by enclosing it within an expanded Marxism: in effect, trying to swallow up the enterprises of Derrida, Foucault, et al. by showing that they are incomplete without a theory of history that only Marxism can provide (and that, when it is provided, reduces them to the level of second-degree or merely critical philosophies). The tremendous compression of Jameson's argument at crucial points derives from this thrust within his argument: he cannot try to subsume poststructuralism and at the same time provide an introduction to its basic assumptions. I do, at appropriate points, try to provide such an introduction and, on the assumption that Jameson will be of interest to any number of readers who have no interest in poststructuralist theory as such, have assumed no prior acquaintance with it. I ask the patience of readers already familiar with poststructuralist thought.

All these sources of obscurity come together, in a sense, in the relation between Jameson and Althusser, for in his own tremendously influential writings Althusser has tried both to solve "the problem of Stalin" and to provide Marx with a "structuralist" reinterpretation that would allow contemporary Marxism to compete on equal terms with various powerful movements in European thought. Here, once again, Jameson's argument is necessarily compressed in the extreme: he cannot move beyond Althusser and simultaneously provide an introductory course in Althusserian Marxism, so he is compelled to assume some background on the part of his readers. This, as my title will perhaps already have suggested, is the background I try most especially to provide. The title *Jameson, Althusser, Marx* is meant not only to trace the line of intellectual descent that runs backward from *The Political Un-*

conscious to *Das Kapital*, but also to signal Althusser's importance as the major mediator between Jameson's experiments in contemporary Marxism and their epochal origins in Marx's own thought.

Finally, the compression of Jameson's argument raises the question of his own originality, which paradoxically does not lie so much in arriving at new ideas as in seeing the possibilities of synthesis in the ideas of others. Even the central idea of the "political unconscious" as Jameson develops it had been outlined by Terry Eagleton some five years before the appearance of *The Political Unconscious,* and the rest of Jameson's argument turns to productive and, often, pyrotechnical use the systems of such thinkers as A. J. Greimas, Northrop Frye, Hans-Georg Gadamer, and Claude Lévi-Strauss. This originality-in-synthesis is a sort, perhaps the only sort, that a committed Marxist must be proud to claim. It has been said that *Capital* contains not one idea original with Marx, and yet the work has not been without a certain influence.

As I have said, the present introduction makes no attempt to substitute for a reading of *The Political Unconscious:* on the contrary, it will have failed in its purpose unless readers, having had some necessary obscurities cleared away by its exposition, then go on to read Jameson for themselves. Toward that end, I have made no attempt to summarize the brilliant series of "readings" that comprise four-fifths of the book: following Jameson through his actual interpretations is the great reward of having grasped the theoretical system he presents in his initial chapter, and it is in aid of such a grasp that I wrote the following. It is my hope that this volume will make accessible to a new and wider range of readers the work of an original and powerful thinker.

I wrote this volume while a Fellow of the Institute for Advanced Studies in the Humanities at Edinburgh University during the academic year 1982–83, and I thank David Daiches, Director of the Institute, and Peter Jones, Convener of its Committee, for the many ways being in residence there was an aid to my work. My reading in Marx, Althusser, and contemporary Marxism began as a theoretical diversion during a year devoted to another project for which I was awarded a fellowship by the John Simon Guggenheim Memorial Foundation, which thus wound up supporting work undreamt of in its philanthropy; needless to say, I am heartily grateful for the support nonetheless. I owe thanks for advice on particular points to Marshall Brown, Linda Dowling, Kit Fine, Russell Goodman, Alastair Fowler, Khachig Tololyan, and Garry Wills.

WILLIAM C. DOWLING

Albuquerque, New Mexico

Jameson, Althusser, Marx

1

Dialectical Thinking

As anyone who has attempted to grasp its argument knows, *The Political Unconscious* is a work that makes few concessions to the uninitiated reader. Several reasons for this have already been mentioned: the density of Jameson's argumentation and the willed opacity of his prose do not arise from intellectual perversity but from the demands of a very ambitious philosophical program, and they are inseparable from its ambition. Yet beyond those immediately obvious obstacles to an easy comprehension of Jameson there is another: understanding the argument of *The Political Unconscious* involves understanding what can only be called a *style* of thinking, a way of viewing culture and society and history that is uniquely his own. It is Jameson's style of thinking that I have chosen to call dialectical.

To describe as dialectical the thinking of a Marxist critic, and perhaps after Raymond Williams the best-known Marxist critic writing in English, may seem to be treading on the margins of tautology, and yet I think there is a real value in describing Jameson's style of thinking that way. For though it is true that Jameson's thought always participates in the philosophical tradition originating with Hegel and running through Marx and Engels to such "hegelian" Marxists as Lukacs and Gramsci, it is also true that Jameson has forged within this tradition a powerful instrument of dialectical analysis that, though he is sure to be imitated sooner or later, so far remains his own. This has to do with Jameson's perfection of what I shall later on be calling negative dialectics, but in the meantime it may explain why I wish to begin not with a systematic exposition of Jameson's theory but with two examples of his style of dialectical analysis.

The first example consists of Jameson's extremely compressed remarks on the history of painting, dropped almost parenthetically—though his main point here will expand to shed a thousand illuminations in a later discussion of Conrad —in the long introductory chapter ("On Interpretation") in which he sets forth the abstract principles of his system. Yet it is typical of Jameson that these few remarks should contain, beneath the surface of several incidental observations on the history of painting, a sustained meditation on human history —or, as Jameson will usually style it, History, the capital H signalling not simply the long record of dominations and oppressions and abominations that is the story of humanity, but also the source of all that misery in a Necessity that in a properly materialist philosophy has the force of fate or doom. To grasp the point of Jameson's remarks on painting is in this sense to grasp his vision of man in history.

The extreme compression of Jameson's remarks, however, means precisely that the outlines of this larger vision are not to be glimpsed directly in his observations on painting, but become visible only when viewed within the context of his total system. In particular, this means that we must begin by relating these few remarks on painting not to actual paintings as they hang in museums or to the history of painting as related in conventional textbooks but to (though this is unstated) a time before painting, a certain golden and irrecoverable moment in the human story when the visual arts did not yet exist.

For paintings and statues and artifacts, like all aesthetic objects in Jameson's view, can only come into existence through a process of alienation and estrangement within human society. In an unfallen social reality there is no painting because there is as yet no need for painting.

The name of this unfallen social reality in traditional Marxism is primitive communism, and Jameson adopts the name so readily that it is easy to miss the sense in which it carries for him a burden of significance that it lacks in previous Marxist philosophy. Jameson's vision of primitive communism, though it begins in the notion of a stage before relations of domination emerged in human society, has clear affinities with the pagan myth of a Golden Age of Saturn in which property was common and slavery or subservience nonexistent, with the Christian myth of the Garden of Eden, even, on a more abstract level, with Hegel's notion of Being as yet unnegated and estranged from its own self-identical nature. Jameson would admit and even welcome these affinities, with the proviso that such myths are (for Marxism) precisely stories told by people living under relations of domination to defuse or "manage" the intolerable contradictions of the societies they inhabit.

Primitive communism is not a myth in the sense that a Golden Age or a Garden of Eden is a myth, then, because it is an actual state of human society directly inferable from the impersonal laws of History; so much is orthodox or traditional Marxism. And it should also be said at once, since primitive communism serves for Jameson so powerful a heuristic function (that is, it is the ideal standard against which he measures all later stages of fragmentation and alienation), that it is for him something actually to be found in the world. In the era of bourgeois capitalism, of course, primitive communism has the status of a near-mythic memory, but it may be glimpsed in the immediate distance behind the remaining tribal societies of the modern age or behind the bodies of myth studied by anthropologists like Lévi-Strauss, and may actually be embodied in a limited and imperilled way in, for instance, the pygmy society that was the famous subject of Colin Turnbull's study *The Forest People.*

Yet the importance of primitive communism for Jameson is less that it now exists in a few remote forest clearings than that it may be posited as a once-universal stage in human existence, and what is in turn significant about this for Jameson as a student of culture is the mode of *perception*, the way of being in the world, that primitive communism may be imagined to represent. Here is Jameson's first crucial point of departure from traditional Marxism, for which primitive communism is significant mainly as an economic stage or mode of production, the state that exists before division of labor emerges (History proper beginning in the moment men set out to hunt while women stay home to cure hides) to set mankind off on the road of precapitalist accumulation that will ultimately generate capitalism. For Jameson, on the other hand, primitive communism is equally important as what Wittgenstein was the first to call a "form of life," and it must be grasped as such to follow his arguments.

Yet this is impossible to imagine directly. There is a moment of what poststructuralism calls aporia here, an irresolvable bind or logical paradox that teases and frustrates the mind with its very irresolvability. For the unhappy fact is that as creatures of History, locked away in the private and separate and lonely worlds of our own consciousness—the separation and the loneliness having been produced by the implacable market forces of a capitalism that constitutes human beings as individual units or "subjects" in order to function *as* a system—we cannot imagine what it would be like, in the purest sense, to think collectively, to perceive the world as a world in which no such thing as individuals or individuality existed, to think not as "a member of a group" but *as the group itself.*

This is the moment of aporia or paradox, then: when I am in a group I cannot conceive of myself, no matter how closely I am bound to its members by ties of love or habit or shared

interest, as thinking "as the group." The best analogy for
what Jameson has in mind for such collective thinking—
an analogy caught in St. Paul's vision of the Christian Church
as a mystical body, and subsequently taken over by mystical
thinkers through Blake and beyond—is the way any individual in this fallen social reality inhabits his or her body. For
there is a sense in which I think of my arms, legs, fingers, toes,
and so on as having an existence apart from me; I recognize,
for instance, that should my left leg be amputated the being
or subject I call "I" would continue to exist. At the same time,
when I use my arm and its hand and fingers to do something,
to hit a tennis ball or pour a glass of milk, I do not think of
myself as giving a command to an Other, but simply as inhabiting my body as my own physical space in the physical reality
of the world.

By the same token, when I say "I ran away" I do not ordi-
narily mean "I gave orders to my body to run away" but something much more like "I-that-am-my-body ran away." If we
could transfer this way of thinking to a social collectivity we
would have something very close to what Jameson means by
primitive communism, a state in which all members of society—men, women, children, young, old, strong, weak—
look out on the nonhuman world from a collective mind that
recognizes no more difference between individual members
of the group than I recognize between my arms, my legs, my
hands, etc. But we cannot in any real sense do this, and indeed (the moment of aporia again) I am using the language
of a fallen social reality even to speak of a "group" here. In
primitive communism as Jameson conceives it no concept of
the group as such could exist, any more than I can consider
my arms, my legs, and other parts of my body a group, as
though I were to say "the whole group of us ran away: my legs
did the pumping, my arms did the flailing, my eyes did the
navigating," etc.

It is only with the emergence of relations of domination,
then, and the underlying economic forces that inexorably

produce them, that there begins the long process of social transformation that brings us at last to the terminal estrangements of late capitalism, each of us locked within the solitary prison of his or her own mind, our minds themselves the effects or products of a global market system that in the name of efficiency or "rationalization" breaks everything down into units and assigns those units an interchangeable value. Yet even in the first moment of estrangement, that first tribal moment when the social collectivity begins to separate into individual members or units, the world loses something of its fullness, its presentness *as* a world, what Jameson will call its richness or its vividness or its color. Thus even the perceptual world is implicated in the newly fallen social reality to which primitive communism gives way.

To speak of the world's losing fullness or vividness or "color" in the fall into alienation and estrangement is to run the risk of sounding merely impressionistic or vaguely mythopoeic, and in fact Jameson runs this risk quite cheerfully, seldom pausing to say just what he means in using such terms. And yet his meaning is perfectly rigorous. Obscurity arises only because the context of such remarks must be reconstructed from points Jameson makes elsewhere and in other connections. Let us begin, then, from the simple intuitive notion that a fragmentation of anything like a "collective mind" must to some degree impoverish the perceptual world for those individual subjects who inhabit the new reality that ensues—to just the degree, let us say, that my loss of sight or hearing or taste must impoverish that fuller reality I knew when my senses were unimpaired. This is part of what Jameson has in mind, but only part.

There is something much more complicated at work as well because, as we shall shortly see in another connection, the fall from primitive communism into alienated or estranged individuality is accompanied for Jameson by an *interior* fragmentation, a process through which the senses become estranged from one another and begin to function autonomously—

in just the same way as individuals in the world ushered in by capitalism will not only function independently but learn to congratulate themselves on their "freedom," "autonomy," and the like—and through which, as well, the various functions or levels of the mind become similarly estranged and independent in their working, with the purely abstract or rational level splitting off from the emotional, the empirical or descriptive faculty alienated from the perception of meaning or value, and so on.

This notion of an interior fragmentation lends Jameson's thought much of its sometimes bewildering complexity, for at least since Kant we have known how inseparable are reality and perception, and Jameson's argument will always demand that we hold in a simultaneous focus a world *objectively* estranged or fragmented and a *perception* of that world, existing in the mutually estranged faculties and senses of the "individual mind," just as powerfully constituted by the alienation of its elements from one another and from the whole. Nor will Jameson allow us the comfort of choosing one process of estrangement over the other, as though, for instance, the fragmented world of our interior perception were merely an irremovable lens through which we were compelled to look out on a world actually coherent and whole. What historical materialism teaches is, to the contrary, that the process of alienation is universal and all-pervasive, and that unless this is understood there is no understanding History as such.

The matter of the world's losing its color, then, must be explained in a way that takes the universality of alienation into account, an explanation that must in turn begin in the interior separation of the purely rational faculty from the rest of the mind in the first fall out of primitive communism, but that will then see in the triumphs of empirical science in the seventeenth century the first great expression of autonomy on the part of that power of abstract reasoning which, along with the rise to dominance of the bourgeoisie and an emergent capitalism, ushered in the era of human history we still inhabit.

In this context Bacon's *Novum Organum* may be read as the declaration of independence of an abstract power of Reason become wholly autonomous, and Galileo, Kepler, Descartes, and Newton as the agents of its new autonomy.

To observe that the world that came into existence with Newton's *Principia* is colorless, then, is to say something at once rigorous and precise. For from classical or Newtonian mechanics to quantum theory and beyond, physics has gained the power of describing the world in abstract or mathematical terms (mathematics being for Jameson the very type of an ideality that can operate only through a denial of concrete reality) only to the degree that it is literally colorless, an endless dance of particles that underlies and sustains this more cluttered reality we inhabit. The same is true, for both Marx and Jameson, of human society as described by economics, whether the "invisible hand" of Adam Smith or contemporary econometrics, where lived transactions among living beings are reconstituted as impersonal market forces that may in turn be rendered in purely mathematical terms. The colorlessness of the world of the empirical sciences, then, is what Jameson has in mind when he envisions the first fall out of primitive communism as beginning the process through which the world begins to be drained of its fullness, its vividness, and its color.

The emergence of painting and the visual arts generally, then, may be partly explained by an interior reorganization of the individual in which the sense of sight or vision separates off from the other senses and becomes autonomous. Yet this does not give us the whole explanation, for the process of alienation or fragmentation that begins in the first fall out of primitive communism must end in that more radical historical process that Jameson, following Lukacs, will call "reification"—that is, the total transformation of the world into a sphere where relations among rational or conscious beings altogether cease and there are left only relations among things.

Once again, Jameson's adoption of this term and concept so closely observes the doctrines of orthodox Marxism that it demands a careful scrutiny to discover just where and how it takes on for him a special meaning.

The actual term "reification" was given by Lukacs to what Max Weber had described as "rationalization," that inexorable process through which the capitalist system breaks the processes of production and distribution down into smaller and more manageable units in the name of a greater and greater efficiency until society as a whole begins to mirror in its structures the lineaments of what began as a process of purely economic specialization. Lukacs elected to rechristen the process, in turn, to signal a dimension of it that Marx had described in vivid and impassioned terms, the terrible grinding forces of a market system in which the labor of human beings became simply one more commodity in a world given over wholly to the production and consumption of commodities, so that men became, in their relations to society and to each other, nothing more than commodities or things. Along with the connotations of a world of "thingness," then, "reification" implies a world from which the human is being eliminated altogether.

Once again, though, this is to conceive of reification primarily as an economic process, and the economic determinism of Marxism as it developed from the Second International to Stalin's emergence in the Soviet Union as its "official" theorist (with strong implications of his infallibility as an interpreter of Marx) was to ensure that this would remain the emphasis of "orthodox" Marxism. And Jameson, once again, wants us to bracket or suspend the economic ("determination by the economy," in Marxist terms) to think about what reification might mean as experienced so to speak from within—that is, not as an underlying economic process but as a mode of experiencing the world. (Not that Jameson in the least wishes to banish the economic; as we shall see, he wants precisely to demonstrate how any such concept as "experiencing the world" is determined by History, and History by the economy "in the last instance.")

What, then, does it mean to experience the world as a sphere from which the merely human is being drained away and all that is left is things or objects and the relations among them? At the level of relations among people, this seems to invoke the kind of example favored by moral philosophers who are attempting to account for the underlying conditions or limits of ethical behavior. Stanley Cavell's notion of "acknowledgment," for instance, seems to turn on just this person/thing or human/nonhuman distinction: if I could plunge an axe into the body of another person with just the same cheerful unconcern as I chop logs for tonight's fire, I would seem to exist outside anything that could be called, even in the most minimal sense, a human community. If I did this to you I would be seeing you, as I saw the log I was chopping for the fire, as a thing.

If there is no urgent need for a regrounding of ethical categories here, it is because we always retain the option of classifying someone who behaves this way with an axe as psychotic and seeing that he gets proper treatment. Yet it was Marx's point that there is already this element of the psychotic in any relation of domination, that the relation of the *servus* to the master in Roman society, of the Negro slave to the plantation owner in America, of the child-laborer (or any laborer) to the factory owner in nineteenth-century Britain, all would have been impossible had not impersonal historical forces been at work to determine that relations among men should give way to relations among things. The note of impassioned moral concern in Jameson's writing, in the face of Marx's scorn for anyone weak enough to entertain a merely "moral" impulse, arises from a terrible sense that this same process of reification is now working its ultimate deformations on humanity as a whole.

Here we have the origin of painting in that fall out of col-

lective consciousness that begins in the disintegration of primitive communism, and then, subsequently, the entire history
of painting in the process that generates the successive stages
of human society and culminates in the stage of late commodity capitalism. In the cave paintings of the old stone age, we
have the first outward expression of that interior reorganization of the individual described earlier, of a visual sense increasingly separate from the other senses and increasingly autonomous in its operations, seeking to complete itself not in a
perception of that full and vivid world perceived as a simultaneity by the "collective mind," but in objects, images on the
walls of caves, existing for the gratification of sight alone.

Though Jameson sketches in the rest of the story in the
barest possible terms, its fuller outlines may be glimpsed.
What is at issue when art produces objects for the sight alone,
for instance, is a process of reification which will turn Nature
itself into an object, and which by the time we get to the eighteenth-century landscape paintings of a Constable or a Gains-
borough will mirror the operations of an emergent capitalism
by transforming the natural setting not only into an object but
also into a commodity, and then not simply in the sense that
landscape paintings are made to be bought and sold but that a
now-autonomous sense of sight "consumes" the visual artifact
precisely by looking at it (as it is displayed to be looked at) as a
"work of art," a commodity or thing.

To explain the dissolution of representational conventions
in the modern period, then, that gradual wavering of representational form in Impressionism, so soon to be succeeded
by Cubism and then the purely abstract forms of modern art,
Jameson need do little more than point to the tremendous ac-
celeration of history that has established capitalism and reification as the dominant forces in the modern world. For in
a world so wholly reified an autonomous sense of sight seeks
as its object an art also grown purely autonomous, painting
that dissolves the fettering constraints of the representational
fiction (the pretense that art was "about" a world of rivers and

mountains and human subjects in their landscape) to give back to sight or vision the "pure" experience of color and form existing solely for their own sake.

There one has, almost as a parable, an example of Jameson's mode of dialectical analysis, one that sets even a few parenthetical remarks on the history of art against the background of a total theory of History from which nothing—the eye that views a painting, the mind that perceives it, the Nature of which it is a formal representation—can ever be exempt. There remains only one final point, the sort of point, as we shall see, that gives Jameson's thinking about human culture a special depth and inclusiveness missing from other Marxist criticism. For, not content to "unmask" painting as the outward symptom of an implacable process of alienation and fragmentation, he will assert as well that it is a glorious compensation for this process, that from Michelangelo to Jackson Pollock art has *also* existed to answer the deepest needs of a humanity for whom the world was being steadily drained of its immediacy and color. (We will later discuss in more detail this insistence that Marxist criticism be a positive as well as a negative enterprise, that it honor what Jameson calls the "utopian" dimension of human culture.)

Jameson's observations on the history of painting, however, although they will serve to establish the groundwork for his discussion of Conrad later in the book, are in no way essential to that system of abstract principles from which his main argument emerges. This is not the case with the second example of Jameson's dialectical thought to which we now turn, his "historicizing" of classical Freudian theory and the Freudian model of the human psyche—or, better perhaps, that model of psychic economy through which Freud sought to explain the deepest workings of the human mind. Here Jameson provides us not just with another example of dialectical thinking but with a powerful moment of preliminary analysis that then opens the way to his own doctrine of a "political unconscious."

To that doctrine we must turn in a later chapter, but first let us follow the steps of the preliminary analysis.

As we might by now expect, a "historicizing" of Freudian psychoanalytic theory must begin in the contention that Freud, far from explaining a "permanent human nature" that somehow exists outside of historical time, was in fact describing precisely those terminal effects of alienation and fragmentation that we have already seen to be the symptoms of existence under capitalism. In a historicizing perspective, then (if one may be permitted so ungainly a phrase), neither the human psyche as Freud studied it nor the theory he developed to explain its dynamics is permanent or timeless; to the emphatic contrary, both are determined by History as such, and until this is understood neither is anything more than an illusion or mirage. (Yet Freud did not just make some avoidable error in supposing that his model of the psyche had a timeless validity: it is the essence of ideological thinking, of which Freudian psychoanalysis is simply one prominent example, to shut out or deny its ultimate grounding in History and Necessity.)

What, then, does it mean to see both Freudian theory and the human psyche as necessarily determined by history? On an immediately obvious level, Jameson wants us to see that the system of family relations on which much of Freud's theory depends (the Oedipus complex, childhood trauma, etc.) is not itself timeless or eternal, that the bourgeois nuclear family that emerges as a private space under an emergent capitalism is inseparable from the workings of the capitalist system. It would make little sense to look for the dynamics of the Freudian family romance in, say, a collective or tribal situation where children existed in a much different relation to a social system within which their parents played a much different role. It is only when the collectivity has disintegrated, in fact, when myth and ritual and the other tokens of a lived community have died out, that the nuclear family is born to mediate between the levels of the private or individual (the newborn child) and the public or social (society as a whole).

Still, this is to historicize Freud at a quite superficial level, for there is a much deeper sense in which psychoanalysis operates only through an utter denial of history, one that has to do with the central place of what Jameson might call a "semiotics of sex" within Freud's system. For Jameson's point is that Freudian theory, despite what Freud may have believed, has as its true object not sexual desire but Desire itself, the primal energy that gives form not only to individual lives but to human society in all its manifestations. To understand why Freud was led to adopt a sexual vocabulary to talk about this energy, then, and why he made sexual desire the center of his explanatory focus, is to understand the degree to which his theory answers not to a permanent or universal human psyche but to historical objects demanding explanation in historical terms.

We are so used to viewing sexual desire and sexual activity as the very type of "natural" phenomena, however, that it demands our getting outside normal categories for a moment to understand what Jameson means when he says that Freudian theory—he has in mind now such features as castration complex, childhood trauma of the "Wolf Man" variety, the psychosexual stages, etc.—draws on the field of sexual desire and activity as an already-constituted semiotic system, a system the elements of which function as signs or symbols of something else. (It was because sex really did function this way in the bourgeois Europe into which he was born, in turn, that Freud was not in any sense guilty of an arbitrary choice of focus; here again we encounter a situation in which a limited or fragmented perception of the world corresponds to a world actually so limited and fragmented.)

How, then, had sex in Freud's society come to function as a semiotic or symbolic system, a "vocabulary" in which the workings of a more primal desire were expressed? A useful analogy is with the process through which such items as

32

clothes or consumer goods may come to express wealth or status within a society, a process that brings to light two essential features: (1) the goods thus chosen have a semiotic rather than a "natural" meaning (a man who buys a Cadillac is buying primarily a symbol, only incidentally a means of getting from point A to point B), and (2) the same desire (to demonstrate wealth and status) could take any number of alternative forms (the potlach, or ritual giveaway, of Indian tribes in the American Northwest, for instance, or the Renaissance patronage of art). The analogy suggests some of the qualities that Freud's "sexual semiotics" has for Jameson.

Still, none of this explains how sex as a "natural" or physiological function comes to assume the symbolic significance it possesses in Freud's system. The answer returns us to that process of alienation from which so many of Jameson's explanations derive: it is the banishment of sexual desire and activity from collective life, a banishment to that private space where they become the stuff of repression and fantasy, that allows every feature of sexual experience to become potentially charged with a semiotic or symbolic significance that in no sense belongs to its role in the merely reproductive existence of human beings. Thus we may glimpse, behind the contingent workings of sexual desire in Freud's system, the more primal presence of Desire itself.

We must not suppose, though, that Jameson wants merely to say, in the manner of various "sexual freedom" advocates of the countercultural years, that sex is a gloriously natural activity that has been distorted by social restraints or whatever. His focus is not on sex as such but on its exclusion from the sphere of collective life, and his most telling analogy is with eating as a physiological need and social event. We are aware, for instance, that eating, even as what Jameson calls an "inner-worldly event" (that is, something acknowledged as such by society in its collective life), may assume a ritual or symbolic significance: from tribal feasts to the unleavened bread of Passover to the bread and wine of Christian com-

33

munion, food and eating have always provided a vocabulary in which the community may celebrate its existence as a community. Yet this is just Jameson's point: so long as eating is seen in the context of collective or social life its symbolic function will always be ballasted by its status as a merely "natural" or banal event, and the gastronomic will not become a sphere of fantasy, repression, and hidden dreads and anxieties.

What does it mean in specific terms to speak of Freudian psychoanalysis as having been founded on sex as a semiotic system? The widespread influence in recent years of Jacques Lacan has made Jameson's point more available to us, for simply by describing the phallus as a "material signifier," for instance—that is, a portion of the anatomy symbolic both for the female who lacks it and for the male who fears its loss —Lacan puts in the foreground the sense in which sex may constitute a field of meaning or significance for the human psyche. Yet this significance was always implicit in Freudian theory: the very notion of a castration complex, for example, implies that at some deeper level I perceive my testicles, as I do not my elbows or my toes, as the symbols of my maleness, to the degree that if I lost them I should perceive myself to have lost my maleness or male identity at the same moment.

Such examples may bring to light the sense in which parts of the anatomy may function as signs or symbols, and thus by implication the way they draw upon sexual desire as a semiotic system, and yet leave untouched the level at which such symbolic power reaches right down into the depths of the psyche. For we are used to thinking of symbols as "mere" symbols: the man who has had his Cadillac repossessed is discomfited, no doubt, but we are aware, and so is he, that he has only lost the transient sign of his wealth and status. Or, to take an example closer to home, I may suffer serious social embarrassment if my ears are cut off, but this is still not the same as if I were to lose my phallus or testicles. It is in the latter case that I feel symbolically impoverished to the point that the symbol of my maleness and my maleness itself have been lost in the same instant.

The credibility of Freudian theory, then, its power to convince us even now that sexual desire operates at so primal a level that events like castration can carry this significance, is not based (except in the last analysis) on an illusion. This is why Jameson so often insists on the fragmentation of the world as well as our perceptions of it, and on the determination of both by History. The parallel in classical Marxist theory is with Marx's view of classical and neoclassical economics; for Marx did not suppose, when he read Adam Smith's description of an economy operating through impersonal forces to ends unforeseen by individuals subject to it, or of those very individuals as *homines economici* motivated solely by considerations of profit, interest, and the rest, that the world was not like this. To the contrary, the world was exactly as the classical economist described it, and its being so was precisely a condition of economics as a new field of study being born.

The error of the classical economists, rather, was in supposing that the impersonal market forces they were describing had a permanent and universal validity, that in the ancient cities of Sumer and the fastnesses of feudal Europe identical forces had been at work but were so far undiscovered. And Freud's error, similarly, was to suppose that the model of the human psyche he constructed in the early twentieth century, together with the semiotics of sexual desire on which he drew, was as universal as humanity itself. For in a Marxist perspective neither model is universal at all, but comes into existence through the quite different process of universaliz*ing* what is merely temporary and historically determined: for Adam Smith or Ricardo, an emergent capitalist economy unrecognized as such, for Freud, the operations of sexual instinct within the fragmented reality of bourgeois society.

As I have said, however, it does not make sense to speak of

35

either Adam Smith or Freud as having committed "errors" here: the blindness or fatal limitations of their respective systems were, quite as much as the systems themselves, determined by History. This is worth insisting on not simply because Jameson insists on it, but also because his insistence marks another of those points of departure from which Jameson moves beyond orthodox or traditional Marxism. For traditional Marxism conceives of the "ideological blindness" of a Smith or a Freud to the limitations of their own systems as a matter of false consciousness merely, while for Jameson, as we shall see in detail later on, it is something altogether more interesting and suggestive, the inevitable consequence of ideologies themselves as strategies of containment.

Jameson does not undertake so extensive an analysis of Freudian theory just because he is fascinated by the way it functions on the ideological level to shut out or deny History, however, but because he has recognized all along beneath its ideological or historically determined surface the workings of a tremendously powerful and original interpretive system. For the genius of Freud in Jameson's view has little to do with the hoary case histories or the body of precepts and practice that passed on to become the institution of organized psychoanalysis. It lies, rather, in Freud's profound insight into the very nature and necessity of interpretation itself, into that permanent condition of our conscious being that makes an inquiry into "meaning" not only natural but unavoidable.

As we shall see, Freud's central importance for Jameson derives from his insight that interpretation is indispensable in any situation where a latent meaning lies hidden behind what is open or expressed or manifest, and that this in turn is always the case when a primal and eternally repressed source of energy (for Freud the individual unconscious, for Jameson the collective or "political" unconscious) exists in a troubled and antagonistic relation to those overt structures (for Freud the mechanism of the conscious, for Jameson culture and ideology viewed as a whole) that exist to hold the repressed at bay or "manage" its threatening eruptions. This is what we glimpse when we have seen that even Freudian theory and its object of analysis were determined by History. We must now proceed to consider the question of History itself.

2

Thinking the Totality

For Jameson, as for anyone writing in the philosophical tradition of Hegel and Marx, the question of the totality is the central issue not only for cultural analysis but also for any attempt whatever to account for the objects of human thought, for quantum physics quite as much as television serials, for Pascal the theorist of mathematical probability quite as much as the Pascal of Port Royal or the *Pensées*. For philosophizing that takes seriously the idea of a totality or human collectivity existing through history must begin and end in the recognition that literally nothing can be conceived to exist outside the limits of human history, and that the limits of history are just as literally the limits of thought itself. The equation at the heart of Jameson's program asserts that the totality is humanity is History, and it holds in no matter what order the terms are rearranged.

Thus baldly asserted, however, the equation is not by any means an easy one to grasp, and by way of examining its wider implications I should like to begin by considering that transitive sense of "thinking" used in the title of this chapter: "thinking the totality," that is, rather than thinking "about" or taking up the notion of the totality. As readers who have made even limited forays into contemporary literary theory will recognize, this is a locution now common in theoretical writing, one taken over directly from the French and assumed by writers who use it to signal a special and indispensable meaning that cannot be gotten at through the more usual idea of "thinking *about* x." Among readers discomfited by and hostile to the newer theory, on the other hand, suspicion is widespread that this un-English (perhaps un-American) phrasing is simply more of the wilful obscurantism of those who have fallen under the baleful influence of structuralism and *la nouvelle critique.*

Yet even an unsympathetic reader may see in a moment's consideration that the notion of "thinking about x" carries with it a large burden of intellectual assumptions, not the least of which (and that precisely the one signalled by the word "about") is that the most normal mode of rational thinking is one where the mind securely inhabits a framework of accepted ideas and looks out from within its customary limits, as one might sit on a porch and watch the boats drifting down a river, at anything that might come along in the shape of anything intellectually new or strange. The "about" in our ordinary way of putting the matter, then, signals nothing other than a barrier of custom or habitude between the mind and any unaccustomed object.

The value of the phrase "to think x," then, will be just that it signals the annulment of any such barrier, announces that certain truths are to be grasped only when the mind allows itself to feel the customary or accepted framework of its thought dissolve or melt away, and with this dissolution finds itself surfacing within a framework altogether new and unfamiliar. Thus when Derrida in *Grammatology* speaks of "thinking the trace," for instance, he is not speaking about a point he has just made or wishes to make but about the dizzying experience of feeling one world of thought—roughly speaking, the entire metaphysical universe based on referential notions of language—dissolve and another take its place. Most often, the hostility that greets the newer theory turns on just this point: to those who have come of age "thinking about x," and who have never allowed themselves the alternative experience of "thinking x," the claims made for the latter inevitably appear as so much foppery.

For all his troubled ambivalence toward such thinkers as Derrida or Deleuze, however, Jameson never allows himself the spurious comfort of supposing that the experience of aporia involved in "thinking x" rather than merely thinking "about" it can be disregarded as somehow hollow or fraudulent. To the contrary, Jameson's claims for Marxism as the "untranscendable horizon" of any other theory, poststructuralist or other, rest not least on his conviction that Marxist analysis has a greater power to produce such a sense of aporia, of the melting away of customary frameworks, than any of its rivals. What I am calling "thinking x" and poststructuralism calls aporia Jameson calls "dialectical shock," and it is the mark of that Marxist thought for which he reserves his deepest admiration—the mark of such writers as Adorno and Althusser—as well as of his own writing at its consistent best.

Nowhere is the necessity of "thinking x" more necessary, in turn, than with the idea of the totality so central to Jameson's variety of Marxist analysis. For here that framework of customary notions within which we normally remain while thinking "about" a new proposition or concept is an experience of the world so deep that we are not likely to think of it as a concept at all, but rather as the prior condition for anything we might then have in the way of an idea or concept. This is the experience of one's own identity as consisting of a separation from everything external to one's consciousness: I am "in here" in my mind, so to speak, and everything that is the external world or universe is precisely what is outside, the entire realm of whatever is or could be "not-me." So the framework of custom I inhabit when I permit myself to think passively "about" such notions as totality is in this case my own consciousness, the "I" that lies prior to my thoughts about anything at all.

So deep is this way of experiencing the world that I am likely to think of my separation from everything else as being the very condition of my individuality, the "I" and the "not-I" as being the primitive and mutually defining terms of my very consciousness. So deep is it, in fact, that I am seldom likely even to recall that this *experience* of the world, something we do not normally think of as rising to the abstract level of the conceptual or philosophical, is in fact buttressed by the metaphysics of that entire tradition called philosophical empiricism, the tradition that runs from Descartes' *cogito* and Locke's *tabula rasa* to Bertrand Russell's modern attempts to found knowledge in "knowledge by acquaintance" and knowledge by acquaintance in a reality innocently perceived by the senses. This is the tradition now so powerfully challenged by structuralism and poststructuralism with their "decentering of the subject," a challenge that Jameson wants to mount still more conclusively in the name of Marxism.

To grasp the significance of this challenge, it is most useful to leave off any pondering of the "I" and the "not-I" as the defining limits of our consciousness and think instead of the world as it appears to us when we are not lost in reflection on such ultimate questions. In practical terms, this means that I raise my eyes from the page of this notebook and gaze around me at a setting (desk, chair, bookshelves, fireplace, curtains, etc.) not identical with my mind. Or I think, perhaps, of the world beyond my windows, the buildings of the city and the landscape of moors and rivers and sea beyond, of stars and galaxies and the mysterious black holes about which I keep reading in my evening newspaper. It is this last perspective, perhaps, that supplies our most persistent notion of an "external" world, for we are disposed to imagine that rivers and trees and stars would go on existing—as in that wonderful moment in *Women in Love*—even should a poison gas pass over during the night and subtract humanity from the universe.

What, then, is the alternative to perceiving the world and our relation to it in these terms? The answer, once again, lies in the philosophical tradition originating with Hegel and translated into materialist terms by Marx, but Jameson chooses neither Hegel nor Marx to establish his own position. He chooses, instead, a quotation from Durkheim, and he accords it such importance that it is allowed to stand as an epigraph to the book as a whole:

> Since the world expressed by the total system of concepts is the world as society represents it to itself, only society can furnish the generalized notions according to which such a world must be represented. . . . Since the universe exists only insofar as it is thought, and since it can be thought totally only by society itself, it takes its place within society, becomes an element of its inner life, and society may thus be seen as that total genus beyond which nothing else exists. The very concept of totality is but the abstract form of the concept of society: that whole which includes all things, that supreme class under which all other classes must be subsumed.

There is, surely, a sense of dialectical shock in this: "Since the universe exists only insofar as it is thought, and since it can be thought totally only by society itself, it takes its place within society, becomes an element of its inner life." For thinking the totality in these terms means nothing less than that the familiar world we are so used to inhabiting begins to waver and dissolve, that the external world of trees and rivers and stars that we imagined to exist independent of us appears now as "an element of the inner life" of human society itself, that the secret of quasars and black holes does not lie at the fringes of the physical universe but deep within that collective mind or intelligence in which the very notion of a physical universe first arose. To think the totality is thus to see in a sudden flash of insight that an adequate notion of society includes even the notion of an external universe, that society must always function as the whole that includes all things, the perimeter beyond which nothing else can exist.

There are several reasons why Jameson allows Durkheim rather than Hegel or Marx to make this point, one of which is made explicit later in his argument: as a nonradical or nonrevolutionary thinker who yet subscribes to the notion of totality, Durkheim provides a perspective (particularly on the utopian vocation of religion and religious myth) that is not available within the tradition of Marxist thought. Yet another reason, I suspect, is that allowing Durkheim to make so eloquent a case for the social totality as an ultimate category illustrates the degree to which the idea, once discovered, possesses an objective or nonideological validity, so that we may glimpse the unexpected sense in which the systems of Hegel and Marx, rather than creating the idea of totality, were created by it. It is, in any case, the power of the idea itself that lies at the heart of Jameson's concerns, and that provides him with the Archimedean point from which he will undertake a reinterpretation both of Hegel and of Marx.

To follow the full thrust of that reinterpretation, though, we shall have to review very briefly the terms on which Hegel and Marx sought in the idea of a totality and "totalizing thought" a means of banishing the harmful illusion of a reality existing independent of the human mind, or of the mind itself as a sphere of consciousness alienated from the reality outside it. For in Hegel's metaphysical program, drawing on Leibnitzean monadology and arising from an immediate critique of a more naive German idealism (Schelling's "night in which all cows are black"), was embodied the first great philosophical solution to the alienation of mind from world. The degree to which this solution was simply taken over by Marx is caught, in turn, in Lenin's famous remark that, ignorant as they were of Hegel, forty years after his death none of the Marxists understood Marx.

The illusion that I look out from the center of my consciousness at a reality separate from my mind is to be banished, for Hegel, by an awareness that my mind and the world independent of it are conceivable only as aspects of an identical reality, that the world is reflected in the mind and the mind in the world only because both are subsumed by a totality that contains within itself all such partial and estranged realities. Yet the notion of an external world set over against the mind or individual consciousness is of course for Hegel a necessary illusion, the result of a negation through which Being lost its original mute self-identity and (with the formation of a world of brute matter) became alienated from itself. So though my mind and the world of rivers and trees it perceives are ultimately aspects of a single Spirit or ideal substance, their present alienation or estrangement from each other is so far real.

Only two features of Hegel's metaphysical system, so bottomless in its ultimate implications, need concern us here. The first is the degree to which Hegel's program was avowedly theological, was seen by him specifically as a regrounding of Christian revelation within the newly glimpsed limits of an intelligible human history. Thus, for instance, God brooding over the abyss becomes in Hegel Being in that moment of identity before its first self-estrangement through negation, and thus the Biblical creation of the universe becomes the process of self-estrangement through which Being splits off from itself into a realm of brute matter, and thus Apocalypse becomes the reconciliation of all contradiction and the abolition of all differences in an Absolute Spirit that, in a last negation of negation, resumes all things into itself. Thus Revelation itself becomes, in Hegel, nothing other than Absolute Spirit rising through human consciousness in its latter stages to consciousness of itself.

The explicitly theological dimension of Hegel's system is important to us, in turn, because it so often gets left out even when Marx's "theological" debt to Hegel is under discussion, and because the line that runs back from *Capital* through He-

44

gel's *Phenomenology of Mind* to the opening words of Genesis is crucial to an understanding of Jameson's originality within Marxist thought. For Hegel, the notion of reality unfolding through its contradictions and rising to ever-higher levels until Spirit at last becomes conscious of itself constituted no new Revelation but only (and here was the originality of Hegelian philosophy as he saw it) Revelation in its *immanent* form, History discovering its own meaning from the inside, humanity grasping itself not as the arbitrary creation of some absent sky-deity but as the Spirit gradually becoming manifest to itself. Here, in language expressly idealistic and implicitly theological, lies the origin of Durkheim's vision of the social totality.

As the path from Genesis to Hegel's metaphysic lies through the notion of an immanent or historically grounded theology, the path from Hegel to Marx, or to such non-Marxian visions of the totality as Durkheim's, lies through a notion of history which was to take on a life independent of Hegel's system. For Hegel could so to speak get his metaphysical results only because his system was idealistic: the ultimate substance is Spirit, and matter or the material universe is only the temporary reflection of Spirit's estrangement from itself. The significant occurrence is that this very idealism committed Hegel to a vision of history that was to remain profoundly influential even when the Hegelian metaphysic had lost its vogue. This vision of history is embodied in classical Marxism, and it lies in the immediate background of Jameson's reinterpretation.

The crucial feature of an immanent analysis of the relationship between mind and world, that is (this is the other feature of Hegel's system that will concern us), is that for all its metaphysical idealism it compels one to view human cultures and their history as part of a total process; this is why political institutions and works of art and social customs so often appear as the varied expression of a single inner essence, and why it seems intelligible or coherent to speak of such entities as a "people" or a "nation" or an "age." Earlier thinkers, notably Herder, had worked through an "organic" vision of human cultures, but it was Hegel who grounded this vision in the notion of the Spirit working itself out through all the concrete manifestations of the world, and thus almost in spite of himself invented a concrete idea of human history that was to detach itself from Hegelian idealism and lead an influential life of its own.

The manner in which Marx was to accomplish this is well known. The central objective of a genuine dialectic, as he conceived it, was to abolish the idealism of Hegel's system and replace it with an analysis of humanity and the world firmly grounded in the impersonal and material laws of historical development, a kind of immanent reasoning that did not depend on any notion of Spirit to explain the unfolding of human history as an intelligible process. Marx's aim was, as he would put it, to throw away the idealistic husk of Hegel's system and retain the rationalist kernel, and this, for Marxists, is what he accomplished in *Capital* and elsewhere, including some sections of the *Grundrisse* and especially those writings that Althusser and his followers term the "works of the break." This replacement of Hegelian idealism with a materialist dialectic is the famous "setting of Hegel on his feet."

In place of the World Spirit, then, Marx sought the secret of historical development in the economy, that level of existence where human life and Necessity—*my* necessity, as a physical or material creature, to obtain enough food to keep me from starving, enough clothing to keep me from freezing to death, etc.—impinge directly on each other. The secret lay, in turn, not merely on the raw level of the economic but in the way the economic determined the particular system of social relations that characterizes each stage of historical development: the relations constituting the capitalist system in which we now live, the feudal system of social relations preceding capitalism, the ancient or slaveholding societies out of which feudalism developed, and so on. In every

46

such system, said Marx, it is an underlying system of economic relations that gives shape to the whole.

What I am here calling successive social systems is, of course, what in both traditional and contemporary Marxism is called the "mode of production"—that is, any social system (including its laws, customs, myths, etc.) viewed as an articulation of underlying economic or property relations. The concept of the mode of production is one of the most earnestly debated issues in contemporary Marxism, and as we shall see a certain view of the issue is central to Jameson's own thinking, but this is not the place to rehearse the terms of that debate. The crucial point for us is that Marx's notion of modes of production gave to the economic "in general" a specific and powerful role in determining the shape of the social totality, that it described in unmistakable terms the way in which the economic level was to determine the course of human history as a whole.

The invariant feature of every mode of production, Marx asserted in the famous passage in volume three of *Capital* which is the locus classicus of the traditional view, is the particular social arrangement through which unpaid surplus labor is "pumped out" of the direct producers by those who own or control the means of production. Here again we find ourselves on the margins of a burning debate, this time the whole controversy surrounding Marx's doctrine of surplus value, but we need not enter that debate to see what Marx had in mind: the way the feudal lord pumps unpaid surplus labor out of the serf who works the land he may not own, or the way the nineteenth-century factory owner pumps unpaid surplus labor out of the worker he employs does much more than explain how a profit materializes where there was none before. It explains the entire system of social relations within which lord and serf, capitalist and worker, exist all unawares.

The power of this simplifying vision to bring into comprehensible order an otherwise bewildering multiplicity of historical facts is extraordinary, and may do much to explain the

tremendous impact of such a tract as *The Communist Manifesto,*
in which its outlines are already apparent. For starting from
the undeniable fact that every society in human history has in-
cluded relations of domination, Marx at a single stroke provided a sort of X-ray with which to gaze through the shifting
appearances of the social surface to an unchanging reality beneath: where men are alive there must exist the means
of keeping them alive—the land where food is grown, the
pastures where animals are fed—and at any stage in history
these are owned by a few people while the rest are excluded
and dependent. In this begins that dynamic of class struggle
which becomes the central principle of historical development.

The manner in which class struggle then expands to become in itself an explanation of history is likewise well known,
and need not concern us here. What does concern us is the
sense in which Marx's particular notion of surplus value and
the relations deriving from it as containing the heart or
"secret" of social and historical development may be viewed
as being a theological principle in disguise, an idea that plays
within classical Marxism just the same role that Absolute
Spirit plays in Hegel, operating as that hidden essence that
may be invoked to explain a world of changing appearances
otherwise unintelligible in their variety and apparent ran-
domness. And if this should turn out to be the case, the power
of Marxism to explain the world would be a theological power
after all.

Not that there is anything wrong with theological explanations of the world, to the power of which no genuinely en-
gaged student of human thought can remain oblivious and
for which Jameson displays a sympathy unexampled in Marxist philosophy. The problem is not that Marx is implicitly
theological—that he offers the Economy as a "secret" of intelligibility in the same spirit that Christianity offers God and
Divine Providence and Hegel offers Absolute Spirit—but

that he does so at the very moment he claims to be annihilating all varieties of idealism, including all theology, in the name of a pure materialism that is manifested within human history as the Economy or economic level. In short, Marx may be viewed as perpetrating an unwitting sleight of hand here, claiming the economic as material because the forces and relations of economic production belong to the material world —the ripening of crops and refining of metals do not take place, after all, in any immaterial world of Spirit—while *within his explanatory system* the economic has the force of an idealist principle of intelligibility.

A great part of the appeal of orthodox Marxism to its revolutionary disciples in our own century may be grasped here: on the one hand those theologies and ideologies in the name of which humans have always been oppressed have been permanently banished; on the other, mankind now possesses a system of thought which gives a total account of reality on materialist and "scientific" grounds. And yet, according to the critique of orthodox Marxism now well under way, theology was never banished in the first place. Jameson has a "revisionist" reading of the well-known passage in "Theses on the Philosophy of History" where Walter Benjamin gives such memorable expression to this very point, but Benjamin is usually taken to be talking about just the situation we have been discussing:

> The story is told of an automaton constructed in such a way that it could play a winning game of chess, answering every move of an opponent with a countermove. A puppet in Turkish attire and with a hookah in its mouth sat before a chess board placed on a large table. A system of mirrors created the illusion that this table was transparent on all sides. Actually, a little hunchback who was an expert chess player sat inside and guided the puppet's hands by means of strings. One can imagine a philosophical counterpart to this device. The puppet called "historical materialism" is to win all the time. It can easily be a match for

anyone if it enlists the services of theology, which today, as we know, is wizened and has to be kept out of sight. (Walter Benjamin, *Illuminations*, ed. Hannah Arendt [London, 1970], p. 255.)

Seventy or eighty years ago, the moral of Benjamin's parable would for orthodox Marxists have been cause for intellectual or theoretical uneasiness only, as pointing out to an ostensible materialism that it had not yet managed to purify itself from the curse of an idealist teleology. Today, the same moral is what gives substance to the claim of the *nouveaux philosophes* that totalitarian oppression was written right into the heart of the Marxist program from the outset. The direct line that according to the *nouveaux philosophes* leads from Hegel to the Gulag does so, that is, as follows: (1) Hegel invents the notion of Absolute Spirit, and with it a teleology of history that is so far harmless as being confined within an idealistic system; (2) Marx then relocates this teleology within History conceived in materialist terms, which so to speak gives it flesh-and-blood force; and (3) the annulment of contradiction at the end of the teleological process becomes, with Stalin or any dictator coming to power as a Communist, an abolition of differences through sheer force. Thus Absolute Spirit becomes the knock at the door, in the name of History, of the secret police.

Jameson's response to so sobering a view of orthodox Marxist teleology is dictated by the nature of his own enterprise, which is cultural analysis and not, at least in any direct sense, political philosophy. So on one level what concerns Jameson about the notion of a theology concealed within historical materialism is, as we shall see in detail in the next chapter, that it permits a treatment of all human culture, including literature and art, as the mere illusory reflection of an underlying economic level. The problem of a "theological" Marxism that makes the Economy the ultimate secret of history is from this perspective that it denies Marxist criticism as Jameson conceives it. On another level, however, the charges brought by the *nouveaux philosophes* and others are terribly real to Jameson, for the "theological" Marxism that denies Jameson's enterprise is the same as that they associate with Stalin and totalitarian terror. So even as he confines himself mainly to cultural analysis Jameson will implicitly be answering this newest critique of Marxist philosophy.

The problem of the totality brings us now to one of Jameson's most important and original philosophical moves, one that draws on Althusserian Marxism but is within the realm of cultural analysis all his own. The move consists in reconceiving the idea of totality in such a way as to circumvent the serious problems associated with a "theological" Marxism. Jameson founds his enterprise, in short, on a conception of the totality not as some concrete and positive vision of history but as an ideal and abstract standard that allows him to expose all partial or limited ideological truths as such. (Though the term "negative dialectic" is usually associated with Adorno, I shall be using it to refer to Jameson's normal mode of analysis, to keep in view the sense in which his notion of the totality is "negative" or without concrete content of its own.) Thus Jameson aims to replace the totality of "theological" Marxism with a totality functioning, as he modestly puts it, as a methodological standard.

As always, Jameson is choosing his terms carefully, yet it would be a mistake to take him wholly at his word here, to see as a mere "methodological standard" a negative vision of the social whole every bit as potent in its way as the positive vision so central to orthodox Marxism. For Jameson's vision of the totality has the same force as those varieties of "negative theology" which insist on the real infinitude and ineffability of a Divinity which must be impoverished and ultimately trivialized by any positive conception of God. God conceived in "positive" terms must on this account always be some version of Blake's Nobodaddy, a petty celestial tyrant with a white beard who gives back the image of those petty minds who worship him; yet the human mind does eternally create its

Nobodaddies, and only by destroying them as they arise may a truer spirit tear away the veil of illusion and glimpse the light of an infinity beyond. The "negative" conception of divinity at issue here is a direct analogue of that "negative totality" in whose name Jameson will unmask all local ideologies to then point to History revealed as an "absent cause."

The real error of a "theological" Marxism from Jameson's point of view is thus that it promised a vision of the social totality that it could not deliver. To unmask such aspects of human culture as law, art, or religion as forms of false consciousness, for instance, as the passive and illusory reflections of a real system of economic relations hidden beneath the surface, is implicitly to suggest that one possesses a true or genuine explanation of the whole, a vision of the totality that can then function as a yardstick against which the partial visions of ideology can be measured. Thus Marxism may expose Christianity as the delusion it is not simply because Marx explained the world in terms that assign theology and religious myth a determinate place, but also because he told a true story about human history and the fate of mankind in comparison with which the story told by Christianity is patently false.

The problem here lies, as will be obvious, in the way traditional Marxism pictures the totality itself, for conceived in materialist terms the totality does not leave room for one to get outside it to attain to a "positive" view of what it is like, and thus to arrive at a teleological account of history through which to triumph over rival teleologies like Christian Providence. Hegel could be allowed a positive vision of the totality just because his was an idealistic system: the Spirit immanent in history and rising to consciousness of itself *is* the totality for Hegel, and there is no contradiction in terms. When Hegel is set on his feet in the name of a rigorous materialism, however, this situation abruptly changes. The change may be described as follows: where as a Hegelian I was in some sense the Spirit immanent in history, I am as a Marxist inside and wholly determined by the totality, and as an aspect of the totality have no chance whatever of getting outside to view the end or meaning of the process of which I am a part.

This is the dilemma that Jameson's negative dialectics aim to resolve. To grasp the nature of the resolution, let us focus in greater detail on the account of Christianity given by orthodox Marxism. As a form of false consciousness or opiate of the oppressed, Christianity is part of the ideological system generated by successive systems of economic domination to neutralize the rebellious tendencies of the workers whose labor actually produces value. This it does, to adopt Nietzsche's terms, through a process of emasculation: by devaluing the real world in which domination takes place (earthly life is probationary merely), by symbolically punishing the oppressors (now seen as being doomed to damnation), and by envisioning eternal salvation beyond this present life of suffering. Thus it is that the medieval serf or the nineteenth-century proletarian is drained of rebellious or revolutionary energies and transformed into a passive instrument of historical forces beyond his control. The hope of revolutionary transformation, then, lies in those impersonal laws of history that exist outside all such delusions of human consciousness.

There is, however, another perspective in which Marxism may view Christianity or any other ideology, as Jameson points out, one indicated by Marx himself in *The Eighteenth Brumaire*. This is to see ideology not as false consciousness but as ideological closure: that is, as the approximation of some truth about the totality that, given the limitations always imposed by the historical process, stands in for the deeper truth it exists to deny. As creatures of the economic systems that enclose them, human beings are forever denied the means of understanding their plight—as we shall see, it is the very essence of systems of domination to hide the truth from those, *both* oppressors and oppressed, who are implicated in them—and yet there remains a drive toward some form of the comprehensibility that alone makes existence tolerable. So it is that in the name of comprehensibility the collective mind

53

invents systems (religions, philosophies, mythologies) that allow it to attain to some notion of coherence.

Every ideology when viewed in this context becomes for Jameson what he will call a "strategy of containment," a means at once of denying those intolerable contradictions that lie hidden beneath the social surface, as intolerable as that Necessity that gives rise to relations of domination in human society, and of constructing on the very ground cleared by such denial a substitute truth that renders existence at least partly bearable. As we shall also see, the notion of strategies of containment applies likewise to works of literature and art, both in the way they incorporate ideology into themselves and in the way the formal unity displayed by works of art represents structural limitation and ideological closure on the aesthetic level, the attempt of art as such to shut out or deny the intolerable reality of History.

Yet Jameson's negative dialectics are nothing as innocent as simply another "approach" in contemporary criticism, for a negative view of the totality provides a means of analyzing all human culture and not just isolated works of art. Thus Hegel's entire philosophical system, for instance, becomes for Jameson simply a grand strategy of containment in itself, born in that same awareness of social tensions and contradictions that would preoccupy Marx a few years later but not yet capable of being resolved in materialist terms. Thus Hegel, deeply disillusioned by the failure of the Napoleonic revolution and yet aware that neither Romantic nostalgia for a more "organic" world nor bourgeois progressivism could provide any genuine solutions, projected the return to Absolute Spirit as that salvation within history in which all contradictions would be reconciled. So the philosophy of the Spirit, for all Hegel's unquestioned importance as Marx's mighty precursor, takes its place among the ideologies of its time.

Among those ideologies we find, as well, Marx's philosophy of history. Though Jameson as a Marxist is too politic to give the matter more than passing mention, it is clear that his notion of ideologies as strategies of containment extends to classical Marxism, to that salvational "story" about the plot of History that is embodied in Marx's writings. The teleology implicit in orthodox Marxism is not, for Jameson, an error imposed on Marx by his later followers, and the economic determinism attacked by the *nouveaux philosophes* and various "revisionist" Marxists is not some vulgar heresy within Marxism. To the contrary, the Hegelian strand in Marx's thought testifies to the extent to which it too was an ideology produced in and determined by its historical situation—the extent, that is, to which even Marx was unable to confront the real terror of a Necessity that turns history into a waking nightmare. Marx's unwitting strategy of containment, his way of holding the nightmare at bay, was thus to tell a providential fable in which the various modes of production generate one another in neat succession until revolution and the withering away of the state are imminently at hand.

The real power of Jameson's negative dialectics may be suggested by the ease with which they find a place for that teleological or "theological" thrust within classical Marxism that so embarrasses many contemporary Marxists. Marx's real genius, for Jameson, lies not in his having devised an elaborate system of salvational history but in his having dug through those layers of accumulated illusion that every previous generation called "history" to a stark confrontation with Necessity itself, that dark and implacable force lying eternally just beyond the borders of any possible vision of human freedom, that baleful power that through all the ages of humanity has been at work to produce relations of domination within society, has led to alienation and fragmentation and estrangement, to our permanent imprisonment within one or another structure of false reality. The endless dismantling of such false structures, a repeated and hopeful gesture in the direction of that Freedom that may ultimately be won from Necessity, will be the distinguishing mark of Jameson's criticism.

Though once again Jameson has been anticipated here by

that Althusserian Marxism whose lessons he has learned so well, there is a parallel between his enterprise and Jacques Lacan's reinterpretation of classical Freudian theory. For Lacan saw that the terror of Freud's discovery of the unconscious was met by its own kind of denial, that constructing an elaborate system of psychoanalytic explanation was one way of domesticating the terror, and that the institution of organized psychoanalysis that survived Freud may be viewed as the biggest repression of all. There is precedent for this sort of purifying or "de-encrustating" vision within Marxism (a tract like Gramsci's *Revolution against Capital* must have sprung from a kindred impulse), and yet nowhere within contemporary Marxism is it pursued with more rigor and intellectual passion than in Jameson's writings.

Those who regard Jameson as a literary critic, that is to say, have hold of about half the truth. He is a literary critic, and he will be treated as such in the following chapters. Yet literature is for him only an occasion—though a privileged one, it may be—for a negative dialectics that eschews the false comfort of any salvational view of history, any "positive" philosophy deriving from a view of the totality which reproduces all the complacent illusions of ideology. The aim of Jameson's critical practice is to tear away the veil of illusion from the social and cultural and historical process and allow us to glimpse the eternal Necessity beyond, and a Freedom that can be won from that Necessity only when all mystification has ceased to exist. On Jameson's account of the totality we can never in direct terms know what History is, but given the prevalence of ideology and illusion we can always know what it is not.

3

The Problem of the Superstructure

The "problem of the superstructure" for Marxist criticism is well known. It is that if the superstructure exists, at least on the terms dictated by orthodox or traditional Marxism, then no such thing as Marxist criticism can exist. There can be, it is true, a kind of mechanical pigeonholing of literary works, as in Christopher Caudwell's crude attempts to demonstrate that literary genres always reflect the economic system in which they are produced, or Lucien Goldmann's more sophisticated proclamation of a "homologous" relationship between the economic and cultural levels of society (we shall have occasion to examine Jameson's response to the latter idea), but there can be no such thing as a criticism that takes literature seriously as representing a sphere of meaning or significance on its own. Since Jameson will settle for nothing less, his enterprise in one aspect may be viewed as an attempt to rescue literature from a narrow Marxist dogmatism.

There has always been some evidence that Marx did not mean exactly what he seemed to be saying when he specified the relation between base and superstructure, between the economic and the cultural, enshrined in orthodox Marxist dogma. Beginning with the hegelian Marxism of Lukacs there have been various attempts to rescue literature from this constricting orthodoxy, the most impressive of which, as we shall see, is Jameson's argument that the concept of a "mode of production" functions in Marxist theory not as an actual description of historical development but as a model for understanding it. Yet to understand the rescue attempt it is first necessary to grasp what it is trying to rescue literature from, which in general terms is the economic determinism of Kautsky and Plekhanov and the Second International. It is fashionable now in contemporary Marxism to claim that the Second International produced only a crude caricature of genuine Marxism, but if so it was a caricature that long passed for the original, and in doing so had a tremendous impact on modern history.

Let us begin, then, with the concept of the superstructure, a concept that has seldom gotten much in the way of full discussion in Marxist analyses of culture and society. Even within orthodox or traditional Marxism, that is, there has often been a tendency to introduce the term "superstructure" and follow it with a few parenthetical examples of what is meant— typically, for instance, "superstructure (law, politics, religion, philosophy, etc.)." The superstructure as Marx conceived it did of course include such institutions as law and religion, such practices or activities as (parliamentary or reformist) politics, such intellectual products as philosophical systems or doctrines, and so on. In any such formulation, though, it is the "etc." that ought to carry the largest burden, for in the superstructure Marx meant to include not just this or that obviously "ideological" dimension of social reality but society as we actually inhabit it. In following the concept through its troubled history in Marxist theory we do not go far wrong if we simply substitute for "superstructure" such a term as "culture" or "society."

The reason the superstructure has been thought of in relation to a few obviously "ideological" institutions like law and religion is not hard to guess, for in these instances it is simple and rhetorically effective to demonstrate that the cultural level simply reflects and furthers the purposes of the system of economic domination functioning beneath the surface. Thus religion, as we have said, becomes a means of emptying the oppressed classes of their rebellious impulses, and thus laws of property protect the interests of those who own the means of production, while the means of enforcing those laws (police, jails, etc.) become instruments of the ruling class. Though on theoretical grounds always scornful of mere "voluntarism" (revolution is guaranteed by the impersonal laws of history, and does not need your help or mine to occur), Marxism has on the practical level always placed a great emphasis on revolutionary activity, and no model of the relation between base and superstructure has been better suited to awaken the proletariat to a sense of its own exploitation.

According to this same model, then, the "base" or "infrastructure"—the two terms are interchangeable in Marxist theory—is that hidden level of reality on which purely economic relations function to determine the shape of society as a whole. As we have seen, the mechanism of this determination was for Marx the specific arrangement according to which, in any society or era of history, those who own the means of production pump unpaid surplus labor out of the direct producers, the peasant working his lord's land or the wage-laborer working in a coal mine or a factory. It is the grim reality of the economic working away beneath the surface of social appearances that produces those relations of production in which a few people live in mansions and a great number in slums, "social appearances" being here simply another name for the superstructure, "the economic" a name for base or infrastructure. This is the context within which the economic determines the cultural as well as the political or institutional, works of art as well as religious doctrines or laws of property.

Still, the model leaves some room for a distinction between

59

the political and the cultural, for property laws represent the system in its coercive aspect, books and movies and television programs being more innocently "ideological" phenomena that simultaneously serve the oppressed classes as opiates and brainwash them into blindly accepting the values of the dominant class. Yet in orthodox Marxism the distinction does not matter very much, for the revolution that brings the proletariat to power will then allow the Party to alter the relations of production in its name, and the superstructure will inevitably be transformed to reflect the new economic reality beneath the surface. (Here, it may be noted, we have the grounds of another contemporary attack on the economic determinism in whose name Stalin came to power, for if the Economy determines everything else the simple abolition of private property makes the totalitarian features of Stalinism—secret police, forced labor, etc.—at most a temporary worry.)

For the Marxist literary or cultural critic, however, there is a real bind here, for the same model of base and superstructure that at least allows such institutions as the legal system some coercive force would seem to have dismissed the merely cultural as not being worth even *that* degree of analysis. A Marxist criticism taking the model seriously, in short, not only must view the entire superstructure as the unreal fabric of appearances projected by an underlying economic reality, but within that context must view art and literature as being more unreal than everything else, epiphenomena of the already epiphenomenal. The orthodox Marxist critic inhabits a world where the *Iliad* and *Hamlet* and *Middlemarch* are illusions that have been conjured away in the name of the Economic, and where (unless one wishes, like Caudwell, to go through the laborious process of proving to be illusory what is already known to be so) there is quite literally nothing left to do.

In addressing this problem, which for him as a Marxist critic is the central problem, Jameson does not mount a direct attack on the crude economic determinism on which the "orthodox" Marxist model so evidently depends. His attack, rather, calculated to associate him with those forces in contemporary Marxism that through an internal critique wish to repudiate Stalinism and Soviet communism generally, will follow the lines of Althusser's brilliant analysis of the ideas of causality implicit in various models of the relationship between base and superstructure. Jameson provides a diagram of the relationship asserted by the "orthodox" model; for purposes of discussion now I offer a much-simplified version:

Superstructure (culture = ideology)

Base or "Infrastructure" (economic relations)

The point of Jameson's diagram is to represent the articulations of the various levels of base and superstructure. My version aims at something more modest, namely, reminding us at the outset that any version of the base-superstructure relation must include some point of contact or "line of impingement" between the two, some place at which the economic touches the cultural or ideological and determines its nature in the direction indicated by the arrows.

Althusser's critique of the orthodox model begins in a scrutiny of this line of impingement, and specifically with the point that the relation between base and superstructure, whenever it is pictured this way, must be *causal.* In fact this must all along have been intuitively obvious to anyone familiar with the orthodox model, for to talk about the way in which the economic "determines" the cultural or ideological must be to invoke some idea of causality, if not of the direct "X causes Y" variety then of some mode that would allow a Marxist analysis to get from the hidden level of economic relations to the visible level of beliefs, customs, institutions, and the rest. Yet this intuitively obvious idea in fact contains a number of problems and difficulties, among them a problem serious enough to dispose of the "orthodox" model in immediate terms.

The most devastating thrust of Althusser's critique, almost peremptory in its force, is against the economic determinism implicit in the orthodox model. For his point is not simply that this model depends precisely on an "X causes Y" notion of causality for its coherence, but also that that notion is necessarily one of *mechanical* causality, the sort associated with one billiard ball hitting and causing the motion of another. Thus Althusser opens up the line of a critique that may be viewed almost in Kantian terms: to the extent that the orthodox model insists on viewing base and superstructure as substances, and the relation between them as one substance acting on another, it cannot on its own terms be true to its object, which is not a substance but a structure of social and institutional relations. Kant's point in a similar context was that theology could not be allowed to go on describing God as pure spirit or immaterial being and then to invoke the notion of material causality to picture him as prime mover or First Cause. The purely negative thrust of Althusser's critique is at a similar logical incoherence at the heart of orthodox Marxism, but its positive consequence for Marxist criticism is that one need no longer try to think of *Hamlet* as the effect of a mechanical cause.

Jameson wholly accepts the consequences of this critique in its main outlines, and his one reservation, characteristically, is less a reservation as such than an attempt to see why the orthodox notion of base and superstructure ever had any plausibility in the first place. And his answer is that on a historically local level we can see ways in which the idea of mechanical causality makes a good deal of sense. Marshall McLuhan's contention that the invention of the printing press—a material invention producing the book as a new kind of material object—had profound effects on human consciousness and society, for instance, retains its intelligibility in the face of Althusser's critique, as does the contention that novelists like Gissing were compelled to change the "inner" or "literary" form of their narratives to accord with certain drastic changes in publishing format at the end of the nineteenth century. When the material or the economic intrudes thus crudely into cultural history, in short, it may serve to remind us of the ultimate roots of everything cultural in History and Necessity.

Yet the primary object of Althusser's critique is not the mechanical causality of the orthodox model, which once perceived for what it is is perhaps too easy a target, but what he variously calls the "expressive causality" or the "historicism" of an alternative model of the relation between base and superstructure, one that arose not least out of a sense of dissatisfaction with the determinism of the Second International. This is a notion of causality associated with a version of Marxist theory we have already discussed in some detail, that teleological or "theological" Marxism that takes over Hegel's Absolute Spirit and simply transforms it into the Economy, an essence at work behind the scenes determining all the phenomena of the surface. As we have seen, this presents problems for Marxist political theory because it is idealistic, transforming Marx into the teller of a salvational story rather than a scientific theorist of historical laws. For Marxist literary or cultural criticism, however, it has somewhat different implications.

In Hegel's original account of the totality, we recall, there always lurked in the background a metaphor of mind and body: the Spirit stood in relation to the material universe as mind to body, and in working itself out through the concrete manifestations of history it took the form, in effect, of a directing intelligence. When the Economy is taken to be the hidden essence behind social or cultural reality, then, something similar occurs: behind art, religion, law, etc., is discernible the infrastructure *expressed through* the elements or instances of the superstructure. The model of interpretation implied here is thus similar to the way we interpret a friend's facial expression, through the elements of which (mouth agape, eyes wide) we may interpret the "state of mind" (shock or surprise) that is their informing essence. The notion of expressive causality thus turns on the notion of an essence expressed by and equally present in every element or feature of a visible system of appearances.

Within Marxism this notion of expressive causality is most closely associated with Lukacs, but as Jameson points out, it is as much at work in the cultural analyses of Spengler or Foucault as in those of Hegel or Lukacs. Whether the historical telos is that of Spenglerian decline or the controlling essence the Foucauldian *épisteme*, in short, all such accounts contain some equivalent of a Zeitgeist that works away behind the various concrete manifestations of history to bring them into comprehensible order. The problem with expressive causality, in turn, may be seen in the idea of "period" or historical epoch it entails: we can, it is true, take up a variety of disparate social phenomena and, positing a hidden essence, turn them into a seamless web. But then (and this is the central weakness of the idea) the unity or "organic wholeness" of a period or epoch will be precisely something we have conjured into existence with the very notion of hidden essence our analysis supplied at the outset.

Beyond the fact that the unity or wholeness thus produced is factitious, however, Jameson sees two particular problems with the idea of expressive causality as attacked by Althusser. The first is that interpreting or analyzing a historical period on such a model must involve an interpretive practice to which, as we shall see in chapter 5, he recognizes strong objections. This is interpretation as *rewriting* in terms of a "master narrative" to bring to light the "meaning" of what is thus interpreted. Thus, to take the example lying closest to hand, if we were to take Marx's providential or salvational account of history as a master narrative, and if we then subscribed to the notion of expressive causality employed by Lukacs, we would possess a means of "rewriting" events, institutions, works of art—everything, in short, in the social and cultural field—in terms of that underlying economic process that is their hidden essence.

The other problem with expressive causality that is brought to light by Althusser's critique, and one especially important to Jameson as a literary or cultural critic, is that associated with *mediation,* or the demonstration that all levels of the superstructure are only superficially different reflections of the same essence. We shall discuss Jameson's position on mediation later in this chapter, but at the moment what is important is that the concept asserts an underlying *identity* between any two levels of the superstructure, and further assumes that any one can (as Jameson will say) be "folded into" the next, and all ultimately into the economic. Thus both the political system and the legal system of a society are not merely illusory reflections of its relations of production, for instance, but each system is ultimately identical with the other and both with the economic in which they have the real source of their unreal existence. For a Marxist literary or cultural criticism this means in an even more conclusive sense that art and literature have no life of their own.

A Marxist criticism becomes possible, then, only when some alternative account of the relation between base and superstructure is given. The most powerful alternative so far proposed is Althusser's notion of "structural causality," the authority of which stands behind Jameson's theory and practice as a literary critic. The idea of structural causality is not easy to grasp, not least because it may seem so strongly to offend against our usual notions of cause and effect. The two notions of causality we have so far discussed illustrate the point perfectly: the idea of mechanical or billiard-ball causality causes us no discomfort, for it *is* in a sense what we are used to meaning by causality, the primitive notion from which all others derive. The Hegelian notion of expressive causality is perhaps less self-evident, but because looking at mind or personality as the hidden cause of human action is so familiar to us, it is comfortable enough. It is because Althusser wishes to describe a form of causality radically dissimilar from either of these, and therefore from what we are used to meaning by causality, that it at first seems altogether foreign.

We may begin, then, by trying to see just why Althusser is committed to so apparently strange a notion of causality. The matter may most usefully be posed in terms of the problem Althusser is attempting to solve: on the one hand his object is to rid his analysis of anything that looks like a hidden essence working away behind the surface of appearances, and on the other he wishes to arrive at an explanation of the structure of social reality which does not appeal to any notion of occult causality to obtain its results. So the problem, as Althusser himself must have grasped it at the outset, must have looked something like this: if we are examining the functional relations among elements of the superstructure (law, religion, politics, etc.) but are prohibited from seeing them as expressions of a hidden essence, how must they then appear to us?

Althusser's philosophical move in this situation, one that is breathtaking when its ultimate implications are grasped, is simply to point out a fact that may hitherto have escaped our notice, and yet was there in front of us all along: namely, that the social structure we are considering *is* a structure, and structures have a logic all their own. So it is not in an essence hidden behind or beneath the surface of things that Althusser will seek the explanation of social reality, but in the *relations among elements* of the superstructure as conceived in classical Marxism. Moreover, Althusser's notion of structural causality will derive from a curious fact about structure itself: that a structure is always more than the sum of its parts. That is, once we add up the elements of a structure and the relations among them we find ourselves confronting a totality that can be seen as such only as it includes something else, and this "something else" is nothing other than structure itself. So Althusser's move is to reconceive the social totality as a structural totality in the strictest sense.

What happens to the notion of causality here? It becomes, as we have already noted, something a bit foreign to our usual ideas of cause and effect, but it can be simply enough illustrated for all that. Consider the following:

a.

b.

The reason we say that (a) is a meaningless scrawl while (b) is a face or the schematic representation of a face is that we recognize in the relations among the elements of (b) a totality that is more than the sum of its parts; what we mean by "face" is not just the relation of the enclosing circle to one of the dots inside it, or of either of these dots to the other, etc., but all these relations simultaneously perceived. To speak of the simultaneity of these relations as the "cause" of the face we see is to put something of a strain on our usual notion of causality, but it is just this strain that Althusser, in the name of banishing all hidden essences, wishes to induce. It is also the alternative notion of causality that Jameson accepts.

In setting forth the idea of structural causality I have so far retained the terms of our earlier discussion, speaking of "relations among elements of the superstructure" and the like. Yet it may at this point be obvious that the term "superstructure" is no longer meaningful, for we are entitled to talk about a superstructure only when we simultaneously imagine a base or infrastructure as the hidden principle of causality, and this is just what Althusser's analysis has taken away. But when the Economy is no longer admitted as the hidden essence behind appearances, what becomes of it? (In particular, what becomes of it for Marxism, for which economic determination "in the last instance" is an article of faith?) Althusser's solution to this problem is characteristically bold: he assigns the economic a place *within* the system of relations comprising the social totality—that is, makes it a part of the social structure along with law, politics, religion, art, and the rest—and by this means banishes forever any notion of the Economy as a hidden essence or occult cause.

Yet this seems to be less a solution than a whole new problem: can a Marxism that views the economic as simply one more level within the social totality properly describe itself as Marxism at all? The manner in which Althusser meets this objection takes us to the heart of his theory, and to the most powerful of his contributions to contemporary social analysis. The answer comes in the form of Althusser's concept of *overdetermination*, which he is correctly supposed to have borrowed from psychoanalysis—ultimately, from Freud's contention that a psychic or neurotic phenomenon may have more than one cause, each sufficient in itself—but which is ultimately made obscure by any attempt to see it as simply a new application of the psychoanalytic concept. Althusserian overdetermination, which must be taken finally on its own conceptual grounds, arises from the notion of a structural totality within which the function of every element is simultaneously a condition for the function of every other.

The concept of overdetermination becomes clearer, perhaps, if we consider an analogy with the human body viewed as a physiological system, and in particular with the heart, as it was long thought of in medicine, poetry, and even philosophy, as the "dominant organ" within that system. On such a view the heart will correspond to the Economy in both the classical and the hegelian versions of the base-superstructure model, and we can immediately see that it makes a kind of sense to view the heart this way. If my heart stops beating one minute from now, it will only be a few more moments until my body as a total system shuts down as well, until my lungs cease to function, my liver and kidneys to work, and so on. In this context it seems natural enough to see the healthy function of my heart as the "underlying condition" of all my other physiological processes, or to exercise and eat wisely in hopes of preventing a heart attack that will kill me.

If we think about it for a moment, though, we will recognize that we are playing a kind of mental trick on ourselves here, that we are making a "dominant instance" out of the fact that coronary function is a sine qua non for other physiological processes, which is something else altogether. What Althusserian overdetermination asks us to see is that this also works in reverse, that (to pursue our analogy) the function of my lungs is equally necessary to my heartbeat (which would stop the moment oxygen ceased to be delivered to my heart), that the simultaneous function of my lungs and heart is necessary to my kidney function (which in turn must continue uninterrupted if my heart and lungs are to keep working), and so on. All of which is to say that in the physiological system I call my body the function of any one thing (liver, kidney, skin, nervous system) assumes the simultaneous function of all the others, thus giving us a systemic or synergistic whole in which the idea of a dominant instance is no longer meaningful.

In purely abstract terms, then, the point of Althusserian overdetermination is to insist that it makes little sense to assign the Economy or "economic determination in the last instance" the role it was made to play in orthodox and hegelian Marxism both, to regard the various levels of the superstructure as mere illusory reflections of underlying relations of production. Yet the positive effect of overdetermination is to give those same superstructural levels a vitality and logic of their own, for to assert that religion or law or politics are not just reflections of but conditions for the functioning of the Economy is to summon into existence a flesh-and-blood world in which men not only labor for wages but also vote and argue and believe, and in which the way they vote or what doctrines they believe does much to shape the economic structure within which they work for wages.

Three important concepts are entailed by Althusser's notion of a structural totality, two of which may be briefly mentioned. The first, one that we will later see to be central to Jameson's theory of interpretation, is the idea of history as an "absent cause." It will be seen that this concept follows directly from Althusser's notion of the totality as a structure: since the idea of structure is purely relational, it can make no sense to talk of any structure as having an existence separate from its elements. When we look at the elements of the "face" represented earlier, for instance, we do not see those elements *and* something apart from them; what we see, rather, is a set of relations among the elements, and it is this we call structure. To speak of history as an "absent cause" is similarly to speak of the structure of the totality as something *immanent in* its elements or effects, not as something that is additional to and apart from them.

The second concept entailed by Althusser's notion of a structural totality is the *relative autonomy* of the levels of the superstructure: that is, the idea that religion, politics, law, art, and the rest function in partial independence of the economic and of each other, and thus exert a reciprocal influence on the functioning of the system as a whole. The notion of a "relative" autonomy is not, as has sometimes been thought, a mere temporizing on Althusser's part with Marxist orthodoxy, but is perfectly rigorous in its own terms. My consciousness at this moment, for instance, is *relatively* autonomous in Althusser's sense: I can think or read or write this sentence without being aware of any physical needs, but the independence of this consciousness from my body is not absolute: deprive me of food and water and at some point the deprivation will affect my consciousness; deprive me of them for longer and I will at some point cease to be conscious at all. My consciousness is only relatively autonomous, then, in the sense that the physiological always has priority; the same relation holds, for Althusser and Jameson, between the various levels of the totality and the brute fact of Necessity as it determines the structure of the whole.

Let us end our consideration of the superstructure and its problems by looking in some detail at the third concept associated with Althusser's notion of structural totality, namely that of *mediation*. As understood in orthodox or classical Marxist theory, mediation is precisely a demonstration that the various levels of the superstructure, as different as they may appear on a cursory or superficial level, are really identical with one another and with the economic level underneath. So a classical Marxist analysis, for instance, might invoke the "master concept" of class interest to demonstrate that the legal system and the political system are identical instruments of ruling-class exploitation—that is, that an exploitative system of economic relations is in this instance "mediated by" the legal and political levels of the superstructure, which to just that extent are identical with it. This, as we might by now expect, is an idea and an interpretive procedure Althusser would like to abolish.

Here, however, we come upon one of Jameson's most important points of departure from Althusser, whose account of mediation he wants to correct in two significant ways by arguing, first, that Althusser without realizing it is not objecting to mediation as such but to something quite different—namely, the concept of *homology*—and, second, that some idea of mediation is indispensable to any mode of social or cultural analysis calling itself Marxist. Althusser's real objection to what he calls mediation, Jameson maintains, is actually an objection to homologies of the sort asserted by Lucien Goldmann in *The Hidden God,* that famous study of Jansenism in which a social situation (Port Royal and its *noblesse de robe*), an ideology (the Jansenist revival of a "pure" Augustinianism), and art (Pascal's *Pensées,* Racine's tragedies) are found to share a structural identity deriving in the last instance from economic and class relations.

The relationship between homology thus asserted and the ideas of economic determinism and expressive causality that Althusser wishes to combat are evident. Homologies of the sort Goldmann asserts are something like a symphony orchestra in which every instrument is simultaneously playing the same theme: to someone unaccustomed to orchestral music the oboe will at first sound different from the flute, and both from the violin, but only a moment's attention is necessary to demonstrate that all are playing the same notes at the same time. The totality as Althusser wishes us to conceive it, in contrast, occurs when the same orchestra plays an actual symphony, a myriad themes and motifs developing in "relative autonomy" from one another, all adding up to that whole, immanent in but not reducible to its effects, called Beethoven's Seventh or Schubert's Ninth.

Even though it might be shown that there is something fundamentally wrong with the idea of homology, however, whether in Goldmann's sophisticated version or Caudwell's less subtle practice, it does not follow that any genuine Marxism can get away from some process of mediation. Nor, *pace* Althusser, does it follow that Marxism should want to, for only through this process can Marxism come to view history and society as a totality, to overcome the false separations and compartmentalizations of life under late capitalism. In particular, it is only through mediation that Marxism can fulfill its unique claim to overcome the false specialization of the bourgeois disciplines, in which the economist looks at things from one point of view, the sociologist from another, the historian from yet a third. Only through mediation, that is, can Marxism demonstrate that these separations do not really exist, that they are *symptoms* of the estrangement and alienation of life under capitalism.

Moreover, the very fact that Marxism can employ the concept of mediation (or, as Jameson will put it for reasons we shall come to shortly, can "practice mediations") goes in its way to show that social life does have a prior existence as a unity or totality. Again there is an analogy with the body, which can for purposes of medical treatment be separated into its constituent elements (the doctor tells me my liver is malfunctioning), just as my psyche can be in the case of psychiatry (my psychiatrist allows me to see that my superego is exerting an intolerable pressure on my consciousness). Yet in any such case these separations assume my prior existence as a unified being: the "me" to whom my doctor talks about its liver or my psychiatrist its superego is the same as-yet undifferentiated "me" that my friend asks about going to a movie tonight. Jameson's point is that mediation works in just this way: it could not be coherent unless the concept of the whole or the totality were first coherent.

Althusser goes wrong, then, according to Jameson, because in directing his attack at expressive causality and homology he fails to recognize a more fundamental truth about mediation, namely, that one cannot talk about differences between cultural or ideological levels without assuming a prior unity, just as one cannot talk about their ultimate identity without assuming some prior difference. Consider, for instance, even the crudest form of Marxist social analysis, one that in the name of an underlying economic reality wishes to demonstrate that under capitalism the legal system and the political system are "the same," as being equally instruments of ruling-class domination and oppression. Jameson's point is that if they were "the same" in any self-evident sense no such demonstration would be called for, that only a prior awareness of the differences between the two systems can make even this rudimentary a practice of mediation necessary in the first place.

On a more sophisticated level, the same is true, though from a reverse perspective, of Althusser's treatment of the various levels of the social structure. When Althusser proclaims the "semi-autonomy" of the religious or the political or the artistic, for instance, he thinks he is insisting on their distance and separation from one another within the totality.

And this is so, but what he does not see is that such insistence makes sense only against the background of some larger identity: there would be no sense in even talking about religion and politics and art this way unless we assumed them already to be related at some fundamental level. This is Jameson's great contribution to the Marxist debate over the superstructure: he wants to retain mediation as the distinguishing mark of Marxist analysis by showing that identity and difference are mutually dependent terms, each able meaningfully to occupy the analytic foreground only as the other provides a background.

Whether or not Jameson's point here proves to hold up under more detailed scrutiny, it draws its strength from a general epistemological insight that has little to do with mediation as such. For the fact is that any discussion of differences does assume the "background identity" Jameson insists on: it makes no sense for you and me to discuss the differences between apples and pears unless the category "fruit" is silently there as the background of our discussion. By the same token, any formal system of taxonomy exists as such only by making this relationship between difference and identity explicit: the magic of the category "mammal" for an intelligent child is that it so unexpectedly serves as a background of identity against which to compare the very obvious differences between "man" and "whale" (or even that it invites such comparison where none had been thought of before).

For Jameson, the sole value of this general epistemological point is the way it allows him to redefine the concept of mediation. If the term "mediation" has been so irretrievably contaminated by its association with cruder or more mechanical forms of Marxist social analysis, he declares at one point, he will cheerfully abandon it: instead of talking about "practicing mediation" when he asserts an essential relation between two or more levels of the social structure, then, let us say that he is *transcoding*, showing that the differences between them are intelligible only against the background of an assumed iden-

74

tity. To use this terminology, we might "transcode" the differences between apples, pears, and oranges in the name of "fruit" as the category against which those differences must always be defined. For Marxism, of course, the category thus silently assumed will be society and the historical process viewed as a totality.

Jameson's innocent suggestion that we merely assent to a change in terminology disguises, however, his last important move with regard to mediation. In his argument, we are asked to see, mediation will no longer refer to something actually present in the base-superstructure relationship—for example, the legal system and the political system, once again, as they "mediate" an underlying system of economic relations —but something used *as an instrument of analysis* by Marxist criticism. To the charge that this is an idealist notion, one that in effect makes mediation or "transcoding" disposable, Jameson can respond by pointing out that any use of such instruments will always and inevitably presuppose the invariant relation between difference and identity, foreground and background, discussed here. The instrument can be used in any specific instance, in short, only because of the ultimate existence of the totality itself: we may dispose of the category "fruit" when we have got done discussing apples and pears and oranges, but what the category "fruit" has stood in for, a generalized identity that must stand as the background to *any* discussion of differences, will never go away. This, the assertion of an ultimate totality in relation to all disparity, is Jameson's solution to the problem of the superstructure.

4

Strategies of Containment

Orthodox or traditional Marxism, we have seen, has always tended to view ideology as a form of false consciousness, a great lie about the world within which people live out their lives of domination and oppression. Thus, for instance, the classical Marxist account of religion: people in every social formation suffer the effects of exploitation, and their natural response is to make up a story to explain their plight to themselves. So Christianity, most notoriously, makes up a story (the Fall) that explains present alienation and unhappiness, and a theology (mortal life as a probation for that eternal life made possible by Christ's sacrifice) that makes them comprehensible in larger terms. This is what Marx had in mind when he described religion as an opiate, mankind's way of deadening itself to the actual sources of its present misery.

Yet we have also seen that in *The Eighteenth Brumaire of Louis Bonaparte,* Marx, writing in the midst of historical upheaval with a penetration that transcended mere theoretical tidiness, gave his own authority to quite a different view of ideology—namely, that it is limits imposed *by the economic itself* that prevents men from seeing the real cause of their present misery, and that thus impells them to invent systems (religions, philosophies, mythologies, etc.) that permit them some form of coherence and comprehensibility. Two features of this alternative view are important to us: (1) though ideology remains an illusion, it is now History itself that prevents men from seeing the source of their misery in History, and (2) the impersonal *laws* of history whose inevitability Marx always emphasized are now restored in full force, after having been weakened by the "orthodox" view. (If ideology were nothing more than false consciousness all one would need to do to end exploitation would be to point out the illusion and thus change the way men think.)

An ideology viewed in this alternative light is a *strategy of containment*, a way of achieving coherence by shutting out the truth about History. If we choose to emphasize, with Marx, the sense in which any such strategy reflects a *limitation* imposed by an underlying economic reality, we will discover that we have not wandered so very far, after all, from the orthodox or traditional view. So religion, for instance, while it is no longer simply a level of the superstructure that passively reflects the hidden economic relations constituting the base, does arise from mankind's attempt to work through to coherence and comprehensibility within the false limits imposed by the economic order it inhabits at the moment. The greater suggestiveness of this alternative view does not lie in its elimination of economic determinism, but in its more complex and dynamic portrayal of a collective mind running up against limits imposed by History.

The notion of ideologies as strategies of containment, and of literature as an ideological production mirroring such strategies at the level of individual works, becomes more suggestive still if we emphasize, with Jameson, ideology not merely as limitation, a premature closing-off of thought to the truth about History, but as the *repression* of those underlying contradictions that have their source in History and Necessity. What Jameson gives us, in short, is an idea of History

77

intolerable to the collective mind, a mind that denies underlying conditions of exploitation and oppression much as the individual consciousness denies or shuts out the dark and primal instinctuality of the unconscious as Freud discovered and described it. Even at this remove, however, Jameson keeps faith with the Marxist doctrine of impersonal historical laws, for what makes such repression necessary is that mankind cannot, through mere volition, do anything about its own misery and alienation: the revolution will not occur because men have changed their minds.

In the interim, the only course left open to the collective mind or consciousness is repression, and the name of that repression for Jameson is the cultural heritage of the West, from Shakespeare and Michelangelo and Mozart down to the most marginalized forms of popular culture (which he will then view as the permanent source of revitalization for "high" culture). In general terms, the mode of analysis this authorizes is clear: one is to point out the actual complex relation between Necessity and the forms of social and cultural life. Yet what is Marxist criticism, in more specific terms, to do with *Paradise Lost* and *Rasselas* and *Ulysses?* Jameson's answer is that these, and literature generally, are to be subjected to *symptomatic analysis,* a mode of interpretation that reveals (1) the specific ways in which they deny or repress History, and (2) what, once brought up out of the nether darkness into the light of rational scrutiny, the History thus denied or repressed looks like.

A risk Jameson runs throughout *The Political Unconscious,* a risk he would inevitably run from inattentive readers did not the difficulty of his style ensure that the book can have no such thing as an inattentive reader, is that in proclaiming a doctrine of "repression of the historical" and a "political" unconscious he might seem to be out to achieve a merely facile or fashionable synthesis of two influential systems of thought, a sort of Gretna Green marriage of Marxian and Freudian analysis. The penetration and originality of Jameson's thinking, however, testify to an opposite state of affairs: what Jameson saw is that the Freudian doctrine of repression could be invoked to liberate or raise to explicitness a conceptual position already powerfully implicit in classical Marxism. Nothing makes this clearer than Marx's own practice of "symptomatic analysis," about which Engels said that the genius of Marx's analysis of history lay in treating as questions what everyone else had thought to be solutions.

The deeper roots of this mode of analysis are, of course, in Hegel, for it mirrors that process whereby in the classic form of the dialectic each synthesis of thesis and antithesis itself becomes a new thesis, waiting in its incompleteness to be brought into opposition to a new antithesis that will then produce unity at a still higher level; the notion that anything offering itself as a solution must in an essential sense be incomplete is taken over by both Marx and Jameson. We have already glanced at the way Marx applied this notion to classical economics, seeing in Adam Smith's "solution" to the problems of price, value, etc. (that is, his notion of an "invisible hand" or impersonal system of market forces which regulates all aspects of economic activity simultaneously) merely a universalized version of an emergent capitalism. What is repressed in the name of "scientific objectivity" is thus the system of domination and oppression that sustains the market economy so described.

Classical and neoclassical economics function as strategies of containment, then, not simply through their premature closure (closing off inquiry before it leads to ultimate questions about history and society) or even through their repression of history (repressing the sense in which the market economy described in their texts could not exist without exploitation and oppression), but through the *way* they accomplish this closure and repression, treating the workings of an emergent capitalism as eternal and objective economic laws. For economists like Smith and Ricardo, the triumph of economics as a new science was to have discovered and described the laws of a timeless and universal system; for Marx, both the market system thus described and such of its intellectual servants as Smith and Ricardo were late arrivals on the historical stage, produced with no little flourish by History itself, and their new "science" was merely a symptom of the way capitalism hides the truth about itself even from those who try to explain it from the inside.

The impossibility of grasping the workings of an economic system from the inside provides the ultimate warrant for Marxist social analysis as a mode of symptomatic analysis. Thus it is economics, once again, which within classical Marxism provides the best-known example, Marx's symptomatic analysis of the "trinity formula" of neoclassical economics. As before, the analysis begins in what Ricardo and his disciples had taken to be a solution: an explanation of the source of economic value in the three factors of land, labor, and capital, each then generating a corresponding kind of income in rent, wages, and interest, respectively. What Marx primarily wanted to show, of course, is that any such formula is only an "ideological" means of disguising the actual source of value in the labor of the direct producer, but two less obvious points are important as well: (1) that such an account reflects the limitations imposed by capitalism on those bourgeois economists who, like Smith or Ricardo, want to explain it from the inside, and (2) that those very limitations then help perpetuate capitalism as a system precisely by hiding its workings from those implicated in it, workers and capitalists alike.

This last point directly bears on what Althusser calls the self-concealment or "self-occultation" of capitalism as a system, by which he intends a final refutation of any notion of ideology as false consciousness merely. Marx had made much the same point in *Capital* under the name of the "fetishism of the commodity," which for this reason has become prominent in recent years as part of Althusser's own expanded theory of ideology. Marx's point, which is essential to the entire philosophy of history implicit in *Capital*, is easily grasped: in a world where there is yet no market and therefore no market value as such, the only form of economic value is use value: the value that an object or product has when I have transformed it from its raw materials through my own labor. Use value, which as an economic concept has its origins in Locke's theory of property, exhibits a moral function in Marx's theory by exposing all other forms of economic value as false, exploitative, and deceptive.

The self-occultation of a market economy, then, that process through which it hides its workings from everyone inside it, begins at just the moment market forces operate to instill a new and false notion of value. Consider, for instance, my economic relation to a pair of shoes in a one-person or Robinson Crusoe economy: with arrows made by hand and arrowheads chipped from flint I kill an animal, which I then skin and quarter; I tan the hide and cut and sew the leather with rawhide thongs, and at the end of a laborious process I own a pair of moccasins that, greased with the fat of the same animal, will see me nicely through the rainy season. So far I inhabit a world of use value only; the market intrudes when I am not Robinson Crusoe but a member of a society where even a rudimentary division of social labor is carried out. If this society contains a maker of arrowheads, say, and if, having made two pairs of moccasins, I exchange one pair for arrowheads, my world has changed utterly.

The reason that so apparently innocent a transaction implies consequences so momentous, of course, is that it must assume the operations of a market system already in place: the number of arrowheads you will give me for my moccasins is not arbitrary—aware that one arrowhead takes three hours to chip into arrow shape and sharpness, you would not give me a thousand for my moccasins, nor would I take only one—and since it is not both you and I must have recognized another kind of value, market or exchange value, at work. Yet in this situation it is not as though some trick had been played on us, as though we had allowed our idea of genuine or use value somehow to be replaced by an illusion called market value; it really is the market, as an impersonal system assigning commodities their worth within a system of exchange, that has begun to determine value now. The falsity is that of the new kind of value, which divorces the worth of objects from the labor that went into their creation and the use to which they may rationally be put, and therefore estranges humanity from itself.

The extreme form of this divorce between labor and value is capitalism, which retains labor as the hidden essence of economic value (it is still the work that goes into transforming raw materials into useful products that is the absolute source of value) but which presents itself to both workers and capitalists in an utterly different light (for in a market economy use value is totally hidden from sight, and it is the visible workings of the market—the price tag on the new car in the showroom—that provide the only measure of value that people are now able to recognize). This is the sense in which people living under capitalism inhabit a world that is not only false but false for reasons built right into the way the system operates. Althusser's contribution was to emphasize that this process of self-occultation or "self-estrangement" (the systematic estrangement of use value from market value) was not simply a by-product of the market economy but one of the primary ways capitalism perpetuates itself.

This insight lies at the heart of Althusser's theory of ideology, which he views as having an intimate relation to the way economic systems in general and capitalism in particular work to conceal their essential operations while presenting to those who inhabit them an illusory appearance of things. Ideology in Althusser's account is simply the way this same process of self-occultation occurs at the level of collective consciousness or thought, not illusion merely but *necessary* illusion produced by the operations of the system itself. Thus ideology, in Althusser's famous formulation, expresses not the relation between men and their real conditions of existence but *the way men live the relation* between themselves and their real conditions of existence. So ideology, far from being false consciousness merely, expresses its own kind of truth.

This is the view of ideology that is in the immediate background of Jameson's brilliant discussions of literary works, and what allows him to accept it as properly Marxist—as something, even, already implicit in Marx's notion of commodity fetishism—is the more complex way in which Althusser embraces historical necessity. For it is not simply that religion, philosophy, art, and the rest now have their own truth as being the ways men collectively think their relation to such "transpersonal" realities as society and history, but that they possess this truth inevitably. For, according to Althusser, no social system could reproduce itself without ideology, and what is always true about ideology is the way it expresses the collective mind within the limits imposed by historical situation. Ideology is not just mystification (that is, something that obscures the real relations of things in the world) but *essential* mystification: one could not imagine a human society without it.

Here we have the theoretical justification for Jameson's practice as a literary critic, which will conceive of literature as being ideological in just this sense, as expressing the way men live their relation to their real conditions of existence, and which will thus look beyond its strategies of containment to its roots in History and Necessity. Yet this does not give us the relation between Jameson and literature merely, but also between Jameson and all other varieties of literary criticism, whether formalist, structuralist, archetypal, Freudian, "vulgar Marxist," or innocently belletristic. For anything that is not a genuine Marxist criticism is for Jameson *also* ideological, and belongs quite as much as literature itself to that essential process of mystification through which social formations reproduce themselves; a non-Marxist criticism must also from this perspective embody some strategy of containment.

In treating both literature and literary criticism as forms of ideology, and therefore equally as the objects of his own analysis, Jameson confounds ordinary categories: critics, after all, are supposed to argue *with* other critics *about* literature, not blithely to treat them as just so much more grist for a dialectical mill. This practice can very often lend to Jameson's best writing a dizzying quality, a mirror-within-mirrors effect the rationale for which Jameson described in a classic article entitled "Metacommentary." Yet for all his virtuosity in the mode, Jameson did not invent metacommentary as such. As we have seen, Marx treated classical economics as ideological in just the sense we have been discussing, and Smith and Ricardo as thinkers whose theories were no less determined by the laws of history than the emergent capitalism they set out to describe; this is precisely why Marx could view classical economics, even granting its ideological character, as possessing its own kind of truth. Jameson's originality lies in having pursued the same insight into the sphere of cultural analysis.

Jameson's first question about any rival critical approach, then, is about what sort of truth it contains, and this is not just intellectual generosity on his part (though he has more of that than one has come to expect not just from Marxist criticism but from any contemporary criticism) but the conscious application of a method he has invented out of his own further ruminations on Althusser's theory of ideology. For it is not just that Jameson, following Althusser, sees both literature and non-Marxist literary criticism as being in some necessary but vague sense ideological, but that he recognizes in their relationship to each other a source of elucidation that may be exploited by a genuinely Marxist criticism. Because literary criticism and literature are produced within an identical set of historical limitations, in short, the specific way in which a critical approach denies or represses History is very often the best guide to the way the literary work it analyzes denies or represses History.

The ultimate aim of a Marxist criticism remains, as always for Jameson, the isolation and dismantling of the strategies of containment embodied in literary works, the opening up of the individual text into that *hors texte* or unspoken (non-*dit*) ground of intolerable contradiction that it cannot acknowledge. Treating rival critical approaches as expressions of ideology does nothing to alter this aim, but simply means that, having themselves been subjected to symptomatic analysis, they may become the instruments of such dismantling. The best example of how this works is Jameson's treatment of the archetypal criticism of Northrop Frye, but since we shall have occasion to discuss his symptomatic analysis of Frye in the next chapter, we may here examine a more limited and self-contained instance, his treatment of the semiotic analysis of A. J. Greimas.

In specific terms, Jameson is interested in the "elementary structure of signification" or "semiotic rectangle" set forth by Greimas and François Rastier in their famous article on the interaction of semiotic constraints, that simple yet endlessly self-complicating system of formal description through which they aim to map out in advance all the possibilities of meaning within any given universe of meaning. Yet though Jameson will turn their system of analysis to brilliant use in a chapter on Balzac, our first question must be about why he would be interested in it in the first place. For semiotic analysis as practiced by Greimas would seem to be the very antithesis of a Marxist or dialectical mode of thought, and Greimas himself the very type of the arid, static, spatializing intelligence that Marxism must view as ideological in the worst possible sense, the sense in which structuralism operates as a denial of historical truth as such. Structuralism viewed in this light becomes, as it was close to becoming in Sartre's eyes, the opiate of the intelligentsia.

By the same token, the semiotic rectangle as Greimas and Rastier describe it, a combinatory system of abstract and mutually defining oppositions and conjunctions, would appear to gain its claims to exhaustiveness only through the most ruthless kind of a priori spatializing. Thus, for instance, the cat-

85

egories of their "social model" of sexual relations (matrimonial relations, "abnormal" relations, "normal" relations, nonmatrimonial relations, placed in "contrary" and "contradictory" relations to one another) allow one to say in advance not just where in this "universe of sociosexual meaning" any form of sexual activity (incest, homosexuality, conjugal love, premarital experimentation, adultery, etc.) will manifest itself, but also what, in abstract terms, those possibilities are. And structural description of this sort gets more complicated but not less orderly when constraints operating at different levels—for example, the economic level (dowries, etc.) or the level of individual values (forms of sexual activity as desirable, feared, etc.)—are reduced to a schematic table of abstract possibilities.

As Jameson observes, a thorough commitment to this sort of description and analysis undoubtedly makes one, and would appear to make Greimas, what Umberto Eco has called an "ontological structuralist"—that is, someone who views the abstract terms and combinatory possibilities as mapping out the actual logical structure of reality, and therefore as having the same sort of timeless validity as logic or mathematics. Again, this is the sort of claim that presents the clearest possible threat to Marxism, for at this level we are no longer dealing with quibbles about "the best approach" but with claims about the nature of reality itself. It is a characteristic mark of Jameson's intellectual assurance that, where so many orthodox or doctrinaire Marxists meet such claims with a preemptive truculence, he takes them seriously and allows them a measure of truth in their own terms.

On the face of it, the claims even of an ontological structuralism (if that is what Greimas's semiotic analysis is) are not absurd. For, first of all, we have learned enough from linguistics to be aware by now that a simple and limited set of elements—the twenty-six letters of the alphabet, the system of English phonemes, etc.—may combine to produce infinite meaning or significance. And then, to take such a model as

Greimas's of sexual relations, sex *does* consist of a limited number of anatomical possibilities; the range of sexual activity can only consist of the (genital and personal) combinations. And finally, none of those combinations has any "meaning" in itself: it is only within the social field that a certain temporary conjunction of anatomical parts can add up to "incest," and this is then the same field within which brute sounds are understood as language and Rolls Royces signify wealth and status. Structuralism is sometimes charged by those who do not understand it with applying a linguistic paradigm to things that are not language, but this is misguided. Language has always been for structuralists simply a prominent instance of the way meaning is constituted out of "non-meaningful elements" within the social field.

If we grant Greimas his claims to semiotic truth, then, we have a particularly "pure" structuralism as it appears before being subjected to Jameson's symptomatic analysis. And since Jameson is more than willing to grant those claims—insists on granting them, in fact, as the first move of his analysis—it is worth noting that Greimas and Rastier conceive of their method as applying not merely to social systems but to literature as well. Thus, for instance, they are able to focus on an asymmetry in the sexual relations between master and servant in the novels of Balzac, sex being from the master's point of view (and according to the three semiotic levels they have previously analyzed) "non-forbidden, desired, and non-harmful," but from the servant girl's point of view "non-permissible, feared, and non-profitable." In this asymmetry, they suggest, begin certain dynamics of Balzac's plots. Jameson will make a much more sophisticated use of semiotic analysis in discussing Balzac, but his warrant for doing so evidently originates here.

The reason Jameson will be able to exploit Greimas's system of semiotic analysis for his own purposes, that is, evidently derives from a specific relationship already established between the semiotic model and the literary text—not, as we are accustomed to say, between "literature" and "life," but between the way both literature and life are organized by systems of meaning or signification. So, on the simplest level, what our neighbor's Rolls Royce "says" about him will also be said about a character in a novel who owns a Rolls Royce; on a more complex level, whatever is true about sexual relations among members of an actual social group will also be true about sexual relations among characters in Balzac's novels, and this to precisely the degree to which such relations are not mere physical or anatomical events but combinations carrying social significance. Semiotic analysis does not dissolve the difference between literature and reality so much as alert us to social reality as an already-constituted field of symbolic meaning.

Here we have the explanation of why Jameson is able to view both literary works (for example, Balzac's novels) and critical methods (for example, Greimas's semiotic analysis) as embodying strategies of containment, and moreover to employ rival critical methods as the instruments of his own literary interpretation. For now it matters less that both are produced within the limits of an identical historical situation than that those limits must always be expressed in terms of available symbolic or structural categories. Sexual relations among characters in Balzac, in short, must always occur within the categories determined by bourgeois social relations (these are, after all, the only categories available to Balzac and his characters, and even to rebel against them would be to reaffirm their existence as categories), which in turn are determined by capitalism as a system of economic relations. For the same reason, analysis by Greimas or any other structuralist can only reproduce these same categories at an abstract or conceptual level, which is why the limitations of the analysis may be taken to reveal the limits within which Balzac's characters live and think.

Structuralism illustrates this point particularly well just because it is so apt to place an emphasis on abstract categories of analysis, thus bringing to light of its own accord those abstract limits with which Jameson as a Marxist is concerned. Yet in the relation between Greimas's semiotic analysis and Balzac's novels we have the general form of the relation between any non-Marxist critical approach and the literary works it sets out to explain or illuminate: what such criticism sees, so to speak, is the patterns common to itself and the text it is explaining; what it cannot see is the sense in which these patterns represent strategies of containment, the denial or repression of History by confining meaning within the abstract limits of some system—for example, of conceptual categories, narrative or aesthetic conventions, social forms or customs, etc.—which permit the spurious comfort of a premature closure.

Jameson's use of Greimas's semiotic rectangle is, however, quite specialized: in brief, he uses it to discover which semiotic possibilities do *not* manifest themselves in the text he is discussing, and then takes those gaps or absences as specific signs of the way the text is denying or repressing History. To examine Jameson's use of Greimas in greater detail would, however, lead us far afield. Since we have already had occasion to discuss Jameson's "historicizing" of Freud, let us take Freudian literary criticism as our example of how his own interpretation will make use of non-Marxist methods and approaches. Any Freudian criticism, obviously enough, must incorporate the same strategy of containment evident in Freudian theory itself, of assigning a timeless validity to certain bourgeois family relations and of not being able to acknowledge the historical origin of that "semiotics of sexual desire" on which such central Freudian notions as sexual trauma, the psychosexual stages, and so on depend.

For Jameson, as we saw, the very possibility of such a sexual semiotics arises only through a historical process of alienation and estrangement in which sex becomes an autonomous activity, something banished from the sphere of collective life to a private space outside it. This is the context in which Freudian theory, not despite but precisely because of the strategy of containment that makes it an ideology, expresses a special truth, for Freud's patients really did experience the workings of sexual desire and neurosis and trauma within the categories described by Freud's theory, these being the only categories (roughly, those of bourgeois social relations under capitalism) available to patient and theorist alike. What manifests itself within experience or thought as a strategy of containment, a means of denying the determination of experience and thought by History, is thus made available only by History itself.

The special validity of Freudian literary criticism follows directly from this, for the same historical process makes available to literature those strategies of containment, now taking the form of narrative and aesthetic patterns, through which History is denied or shut out by individual works. Should Freudian criticism prove able to cast genuine illumination on the dynamics of sexual desire in the novels of Dickens or Flaubert or Gissing, then, it will be precisely because the categories of thought and experience available to those novelists and their characters were the same ones available to Freud when he was formulating psychoanalytic theory: patient and psychoanalyst, novelist and character, all inhabit equally an estranged and fragmented world that can exist *as* a world only by denying its basis in the intolerable contradictions of history. So a properly Marxist approach to literature will not consist of denying Freudian criticism its insights, but of showing that the limits of those insights are the identical limits within which the characters of Dickens or Gissing live their lives.

At the same time, the special illuminations afforded by Freudian criticism are illuminations still at a relatively superficial level, superficial not in a pejorative sense but in the sense that there are matters of deep structure which such criticism must leave untouched. Here is where Jameson's symptomatic analysis of non-Marxist approaches assumes a crucial importance to his own theory and practice, for it allows him to demonstrate that such analysis extends well beyond the obviously "ideological" to the most basic categories of conventional thought. On one level, symptomatic analysis is able to show that critical approaches usually assumed to be in competition with one another—the Freudian, formalist, archetypal, etc.—share at the deep level an identical set of assumptions; on another, it is able to suggest that they do so because on that level they deny History in an identical way.

Let us look one last time, for instance, at Freudian psychoanalytic theory, this time with the deeper possibilities of a Marxian symptomatic analysis in mind. Here we shall want to gaze past the furniture of the theory, the machinery of ego, superego, and the rest, the vocabulary of sexual trauma or anxiety, to the arena of conflict it assumes: namely, the individual person or individual psyche. The crucial point about the individual psyche for Jameson is that it is not within Freudian theory itself a theoretical category; on the contrary, it is something the existence of which had to be assumed before theorizing could even begin. Thus the existence of individuals is for psychoanalysis, as it is for most of us in everyday life, something that is timelessly and universally true about the world. Only Marxism, perhaps, which is committed in advance to proving that the timeless does not exist, that everything within history is determined by History, would dream of thinking otherwise.

Yet the category of individual identity or the individual psyche did not need to wait for a Marxist analysis to be called into question, for even within psychoanalysis certain problems kept coming to light. Indeed, as Jameson observes, the entire theoretical program of Jacques Lacan may be said to have begun in a "problematics of individuality" that arose from Freud's untroubled acceptance of individual identity as an ultimate category. In particular, Lacan's insight that individuals constitute themselves as such only through insertion into an already-existing symbolic order—as when I learn as

an infant that the pronoun "I" may be used to mark out a difference between me and the rest of the world, thus assuming
my "individuality" by inserting myself into an abstract slot in a
grammatical or linguistic system—may be taken as the most
radical motivation for his famous "return to Freud"; the same
insight doubtless explains Lacan's great influence on Althusser's "structural" Marxism, and indirectly on Jameson's doctrine of a political unconscious.

As we have seen, Marxism already knew all this, for the
story of history for Marxism, and especially for Jameson's
Marxism, is the story of a fall out of collective life and consciousness into a world of estrangement and separation and
alienation. Only toward the end of that story, when the enormous power of capitalism to break human life up into ever
more estranged and isolated units has begun to be felt in its
full force, when all the forms of collective unity have been sys-
tematically undermined and human life shivers within the
lonely monad of each isolated consciousness, does "individual
identity" as such become a primary category within thought.
To treat the "I," the feeling or experience of individual identity, as a primal datum or ontological category is thus to repress or deny History itself, and what a Marxian symptomatic
analysis will demonstrate is that Freud's entire system is based
on just this repression or denial.

We understand the deepest implications of symptomatic
analysis, however, only when we have seen that the category
of personal identity is not granted this timeless and universal
status only within Freudian theory and literary criticism, but
also within virtually every critical approach with which Freudian criticism is usually assumed to compete. For it is individual identity that formalist criticism honors in structural terms
in the name of such concepts as "narrator," "character,"
"point of view," and the like, and even archetypal and structuralist criticism, with their far greater emphasis on the abstract operations of various systems, retain the category for
purposes of analysis. Indeed, even previous Marxist criticism

at its most brilliant, as in Lukacs's great essays on realism, obliquely honors individual identity by regarding social classes like the bourgeoisie and the proletariat as "collective characters" within that "story" or salvational account of history told by Marx.

As Jameson's deep admiration for Lukacs might suggest, the aim of symptomatic analysis is never merely to bring to light or "unmask" such strategies of containment as the category of individual identity, to point an accusing dialectical finger at their denial or repression of History. For Jameson's ultimate point is that such strategies of containment are inevitably inscribed in cultural texts and our ways of thinking about them—into, even, the texts of Marx himself, who in this sense denied History even as he was instructing the world in the consequences of such denial. The notion of conceptual categories or aesthetic conventions or social forms as strategies of containment is not meant to liberate us from History, but to liberate us by insisting that we are always and inevitably inside it.

5

Narrative and Interpretation

A glance at the subtitle of *The Political Unconscious, Narrative as a Socially Symbolic Act,* is enough to suggest that narrative will be at the heart of Jameson's enterprise, but no title or subtitle can suggest why it should be so crucial to him. An educated guess, perhaps, would be that his primary interest as a Marxist lies in the novel, the one great literary form that grew up together with capitalism and that permits itself to be read, as in Lukacs's criticism, as an allegory of class relations within the capitalist order. To a degree this is so. Though he begins his actual treatment of literature with a chapter on romance that includes brilliant observations on medieval versions of the form, Jameson's real interests lie in the nineteenth-century novel and its modernist successors, in Stendal and Balzac and Gissing and Conrad and beyond. So his interest in narrative is partly due to the novel's being a narrative form.

On a deeper level, though, Jameson's work assumes as its background a good deal of serious thinking that has gone on in recent years about narrative, and narrative not just as it is found in literature but outside it as well. For one of the most suggestive insights of the newer literary theory is that narrative or "story" is not specifically a literary form: it is found, to be sure, in novels and epic poems, but it is also found in movies and comic strips and ballets and puppet shows and anecdotes told at cocktail parties, and to see that it has in all these instances certain invariant structural features is to leave behind the confines of literary criticism for a wider field of inquiry. The narrative form of nineteenth-century novels may thus be taken as evidence of their possessing a more universal dimension.

As we have seen, Marxism in general and Jameson in particular have a deep distrust of anything pretending to timeless or universal significance, and this may well be why Jameson never pauses to reflect on narrative as such, but in fact many of his insights depend on the notion that narrative, once floated loose from its instantiation in novels or myths or epic poems, is really not so much a literary form or structure as an epistemological category. Like the Kantian concepts of space and time, that is, narrative may be taken not as a feature of our experience but as one of the abstract or "empty" coordinates within which we come to know the world, a contentless form that our perception imposes on the raw flux of reality, giving it, even as we perceive, the comprehensible order we call experience. This is not to make the conventional claim that we make up stories about the world to understand it, but the much more radical claim that the world comes to us in the shape of stories.

As one can often get students to see how the Kantian categories "work" by asking them to try to imagine the world without space and time—or, in Wittgenstein's variation, to try to imagine a spatio-temporal object like a table *outside* space and time—one can grasp the full implications of what might be called the narratological claim by trying to think of the world as it would exist outside narrative. Since we are so used to thinking of stories as something disposable, something within the boundaries of the world, this does not at first sound difficult at all, but a brief experiment will show that

95

anything we try to substitute for a story is, on closer examination, likely to be another sort of story. The exercise soon leads, in fact, out of the linguistic and cultural sphere and into the sciences, where physicists "tell stories" about subatomic particles (Bertrand Russell's point that electrons "have histories" depends on this) and where even mathematical proofs, with one step following another toward an inevitable conclusion, exhibit something of the dynamics of plot and closure.

The serious challenge that has arisen within historiography in recent years to old-fashioned "narrative history" may thus be regarded not as an attempt to escape narrative itself —which would on this account be impossible—but simply to move from one narrative mode (kings, battles, riots, elections, etc.) to another. The account of the Mediterranean world given by Braudel, with its long, slow, magnificent sweep of geological changes, trade routes, and the rest is, as has often enough been pointed out, no less a story than the histories it aimed to correct or replace, but simply a story on a different scale, and the same will be true of other *Annales* historians or, in the United States and Britain, of the "cliometricians" who favor quantitative methods. This is why Jameson will be so singularly unembarrassed by the claim that Marx in the guise of presenting a theory of history was telling a story, or that his story, under Hegel's inspiration, clearly exhibits a providential plot: taking history seriously means accepting some story as the means of knowing anything at all.

Jameson's argument in *The Political Unconscious* depends in a number of ways on the claim that narrative is really an epistemological category traditionally mistaken for a literary form, but only one way can be discussed here: namely, the related and subordinate claim that anything (a structure, a form, a category) that presents itself as existing outside the boundaries of some story can do so only through a kind of fiction. Thus lyric, for instance, which in discussions of literary genre is usually opposed to narrative on the grounds that it tells no story but simply shows a moment in which a single speaker utters his thoughts, must ultimately be viewed as a narrative mode. For not only do the speaker and his thoughts have a history (that is, they are part of a larger story assumed by the lyric moment) but we must be able to infer a good part of this prior history if any lyric is to be comprehensible: "They Flee From Me," for instance, is not just the speaker's present disillusionment but the whole story of betrayal it presupposes.

Literary criticism in recent years has grown more sympathetic to such claims as these, at least as they are heard by younger critics who are able to take seriously poststructuralist theories of intertextuality, but for Jameson they are claims that go far beyond literature. Thus, for instance, he is able to show that the Althusserian account of a "mode of production," which has usually been taken to give a purely structural account of social systems—that is, to describe feudalism, capitalism, etc., as *structures* of social relations—is unintelligible, like a lyric poem, except when conceived as part of a larger history: not only does a mode of production project a "story" stretching out to either side of it, but this story is written right into its form as a structure or system of relations. This is a very powerful claim: where orthodox Marxism asserts the priority of the diachronic (historical explanation) over the synchronic (structural explanation) on the general grounds that Marx's was a historical theory, Jameson does so on the grounds that the diachronic has priority as being narrative in form. Structures, that is to say, may be abundantly useful as conceptual fictions, but reality comes to us in the form of its stories.

Along with the phenomenon of narrative there arises the problem of interpretation, and one of Jameson's points will be that the two are inseparable. Since Jameson's views on interpretation are extraordinarily complex, this point is easily lost or passed by. As we shall see shortly, for instance, much of Jameson's energies must on the one hand go to defending his own practice against the claim that interpretation always and inevitably impoverishes some lived reality, and that the question "What does it mean?" is always an invitation to abet such impoverishment. On the other hand, Jameson will wish to lay a great emphasis on the distinction between manifest meaning and latent content that Freud's model of interpretation, and his own as it turns Freud to dialectical use, so strongly insists on. With so many claims and counterclaims in the air, it is easy to miss the point that narrative, just by being narrative, always demands interpretation.

Understanding narrative forms like the parables of the New Testament, for instance, seems to depend on something like this point. The parable of the prodigal son, we are told, is not just a story about a young man who leaves home, squanders his inheritance in dissipation in a foreign land, and returns to encounter not recrimination but a father who slaughters a fatted calf in joy at his return. It is a story about the alienation of the soul from God, about the miraculous existence of infinite mercy when nothing like mercy had even to exist. The foreign land, we are told, is the very image of the soul's alienation from the divine, the killing of the calf that had been fattening for a later feast the very image of God's joy at the rebirth of a soul previously lost to Him. This is allegory, certainly, but it seems to be allegory demanded by the story itself, a second story without which the first seems curiously incomplete.

The claim that narrative always demands interpretation, then, seems to work out to a claim that narrative form has something like the distinction between manifest and latent meaning written into it — that what is manifestly happening, for instance, is the slaughtering of a fatted calf, but that this image "contains" another meaning as its latent or hidden content. Associated with this are are certain other problems long since seen to derive from narrative form as such: that, for instance, every narrative simultaneously *presents* and *represents* a world, that is, simultaneously creates or makes up a reality and asserts that it stands independent of that same reality. Or, similarly, that narrative seems at once to reveal or illuminate a world (we gaze through the prodigal son story to a divine world of infinite mercy) and to hide or distort it (the mystery of God and his mercy can scarcely be adequately conveyed in stories about fathers, sons, and calves). Simply in dealing with narrative, it seems, we are already dealing with a complex and tangled realm of meaning that demands interpretation.

Just as important, the sort of interpretation demanded by narrative has in Jameson's view a natural priority over other modes of explanation. The claim is once again epistemological at bottom: since Reality comes to us in narrative form—not just as literary narratives, but as religious mythologies, theories of history, and the like—it demands to be interpreted as such. Obliquely, Jameson is here contesting any claim to ultimate truth that might be made by the empirical sciences (in which, presumably, explanation takes the nonnarrative form of experiment and hypothesis) and positivist philosophy, but even more obliquely he is contesting the claims of that "scientific" Marxism that sought, in a nineteenth-century infatuation with the methods of the physical sciences, to ground Marxist theory in a vulgar empiricism. Jameson's views on interpretation thus amount to a quiet repudiation of this strain in Marxist thought, from Engels's "dialectics of nature" to the Lysenko affair.

It is the unlikely question of narrative itself, therefore, of problems of meaning and interpretation normally assumed to be the rarefied and marginal concerns of literary critics, that contains the clue to Jameson's posture as a Marxist thinker. For literary criticism in bourgeois terms is very obviously a marginal activity, literature itself being at most a polite accomplishment or leisure pastime, but from a Marxist perspective it would appear to be even more so, the very type of apolitical or "unrevolutionary" speculation. We have already seen part of Jameson's answer to this charge: it derives from an erroneous notion of ideology and the superstructure, and thus from a failure to perceive the cultural sphere as an arena of class struggle and revolutionary conflict. Jameson's view of narrative completes his response: since History comes to us encoded in narrative form, the literary critic confronting a text is, far from being a marginal figure, the very type of the mind confronting Reality, and interpretation is the form of its understanding. The task of Marxist thought is thus not to forswear interpretation, but to rescue it from the denial and repression of History.

This is the ground from which Jameson moves to meet the challenge, very powerfully developed in recent years in post-structuralist France, to interpretation itself, and specifically to the charge that the question "What does it mean?" asked about an action, a dream, a poem, must inevitably lead to the impoverishment of some lived experience. Since the anti-interpretive current in French thought has run so strongly in recent years, Jameson might have chosen any number of thinkers as symbolic antagonists; for strategic reasons, those he chooses are Gilles Deleuze and Félix Guattari, the one among the foremost modern interpreters of Nietzsche's thought, the other a psychoanalyst, together the authors of a projected work, *Capitalism and Schizophrenia,* of which the first volume, *The Anti-Oedipus,* has so far appeared. It is a passage from *The Anti-Oedipus* that Jameson allows to summarize the case against interpretation.

As the title of the work suggests, Deleuze and Guattari choose Freudian psychoanalysis as the type or model of interpretation as such, interpretation-as-impoverishment being precisely what happens when the lived complexity of a patient's life is "rewritten" within the strategically confined limits of the Freudian "family romance" (here, the Oedipus complex, psychosexual stages, etc., as they are implied by a *story* about the relations between child and parents) which is then triumphantly produced as the latent or hidden "meaning" of the patient's experiences. As will be evident even from so compressed an account, any critique of psychoanalysis as such is nearly incidental here: what is being attacked is the numbing reductiveness of all schemes that in this manner seek to limit and thus impoverish a complex reality in the name of interpretation.

As a generalized attack on interpretation, Deleuze and Guattari's gains a great deal of force from being directed at Freudian psychoanalysis as a prominent instance of the impoverishment they have in mind: the image of a patient being inveigled into seeing the "meaning" of a dream, and therefore of the workings of his psyche and the structure of his experience, contains a poignancy that does no harm to their case. As Jameson makes clear, though, it is the abstract model of interpretation visible behind Freudian practice that gives the attack its real force: is not interpretation, as an answer to the question "What does it mean?", always and inevitably the rewriting of some complex reality in terms of a "master code" or "master narrative" which is then given as the "meaning" of what is interpreted? And does not this rewriting, always as reductive as the rewriting of individual experience in terms of the Freudian "family romance," always impoverish what it pretends to explain?

The threat here to orthodox Marxism, which has always sought to explain the "meaning" of everything from political events to cultural artifacts by rewriting or allegorizing them in terms of Marx's own providential account of history, is abundantly clear. And a still deeper threat is posed by the nietzschean thrust of Deleuze and Guattari's argument, which perceives in *all* explanation or interpretation an expression of the nietzschean will to power, an attempt to dominate, weaken, and ultimately destroy all as-yet unconfined reality by confining it within predetermined conceptual limits. In this Deleuze and Guattari are at one with Michel Foucault and the *nouveaux philosophes*, who see in Marxism a prime example of an intellectual (or "interpretive") system that inevitably transforms itself into an instrument of political and physical domination. From Hegel's Absolute Spirit, once again, to Stalin's Gulag: in taking on *The Anti-Oedipus* Jameson is taking on, in the guise of a generalized attack on interpretation, some of the most formidable contemporary opposition to Marxist theory.

At the same time, there is a more fundamental sense in

which Deleuze and Guattari cannot really be attacking interpretation as such, lest they take away the ground on which they stand as they argue. This indeed is the problem of any purely "negative" program, of which Nietzsche's coruscating antisystem stands as the modern type: if such a program is merely parasitic on the positive system it aims to demolish, its truth is to that extent derivative and itself parasitic; if not, it is not clear on what positive or nonparasitic ground such a system could stand. An awareness of this problem explains Deleuze and Guattari's insistence that their attack is *not* on interpretation as such, but on "transcendent" interpretation, this being a general name for all interpretation that gives the "meaning" of its object by rewriting some primary reality in terms of a master code or master narrative. Transcendent interpretation is transcendent by virtue, as used to be said in critical theory, of "going outside the text" to found its significance on some extratextual set of norms.

Against this notion of transcendent interpretation, Deleuze and Guattari counterpose their demand for an *immanent* interpretation, a mode of analysis that respects the internal norms and values, and the complexity as it is given, of the reality to be interpreted. Jameson does not go into the relation between this demand for immanent interpretation and Deleuze and Guattari's own program, which in the name of the "body without organs" and an extraordinary nietzschean vision of the world as flimsy appearances thrown up by a ceaseless material flux opposes Freud's theory of the unconscious with their own purely functional theory. Making only oblique references to the notion of the "schizophrenic text" as it follows from these nietzschean doctrines, Jameson meets the demand of *The Anti-Oedipus* for an immanent interpretation on quite different grounds of his own choosing.

Though it is in the nature of a sidestep, Jameson's refusal to meet Deleuze and Guattari on their own ground here is not an attempt to dodge the issue of immanent interpretation; it is, rather, a flanking maneuver, undertaken for reasons we shall go into in a moment. Yet as we observe him making the maneuver, it is well to be aware of what issues hang in the balance. The nietzschean demand for immanence is particularly embarrassing to Marxist criticism precisely because Marxism has strong claims to being *the* mode of immanent interpretation, analysis which, operating under the sign of History and the social totality, is the very antithesis of transcendent interpretation. A demonstration that traditional Marxism has always been transcendent, then, in the sense that it has produced "meaning" by allegorizing in terms of the master code provided by Marx, is sufficiently embarrassing; what is positively painful is the further sense in which this takes away from Marxism any claims to an immanent approach to reality.

Jameson's flanking maneuver here is to redirect the argument back into the relatively harmless confines of critical theory (that is, of standard debates about literature and literary criticism rather than more obviously "political" issues) and, beyond that, to focus on critical formalism by making it the test case of all claims to "immanent interpretation" as such. Jameson's target, then, is in general all varieties of formalist interpretation—in which category he would include, along with such self-confessed candidates as the Russian formalists, both structuralism and the poststructuralist practice of such writers as Barthes and Derrida—and in particular the New Criticism of his own American intellectual tradition, that immensely influential critical approach, developed by Wellek and Brooks and Wimsatt and others in the 1950s, which came to dominance in the name of "the literary study of literature" or studying literary works as self-contained worlds in themselves.

What keeps Jameson's move here from being more than a simple non sequitur is that his analysis of New Criticism is authorized by Deleuze and Guattari themselves. The reasoning goes something like this: (1) if Deleuze and Guattari are right that "transcendent" interpretation is that which allegorizes in terms of a master code, and (2) if New Criticism, proclaiming itself and widely taken to be an immanent mode of interpretation, allegorizes in this way, then (3) the very notion of immanent criticism, and of the immanent-transcendent opposition on which it is based, may be shown to be a mirage after all. Thus Jameson will at one and the same time answer Deleuze and Guattari and "unmask" that still-influential critical formalism that, in the United States at least, remains a thorn in the side of any "political" interpretation of literature. There is a tremendous economy of argument at work here.

Yet it should not be supposed that Jameson, in shifting the focus of his argument from Deleuze and Guattari to critical formalism, is taking on an easier antagonist. Indeed, the long success of New Criticism in blocking the "political" interpretation of literature in American universities derives directly from its claims to immanent interpretation. The essential claim of the New Criticism was that literary comprehension becomes possible only in the moment when all beliefs or doctrines external to the text are suspended and literary works are read exclusively in terms of their own norms and values. Thus, for instance, not only does it make no sense, when we are reading *Hamlet,* to object that there are no such things as ghosts, but if we persist in such objections (that is, if we genuinely allow our disbelief in ghosts to determine our total view of reality at all times) we close ourselves off from *Hamlet* as a world obeying its own laws and its own logic. If its own claims to immanence may be taken seriously, it is difficult to see where formalism has gone wrong here.

The usual claim of Marxist and other "political" approaches to literature is that the New Criticism went wrong by providing a form of escapism—in Jameson's terms, by denying or repressing History. Yet this objection has force only if one is prepared beforehand to accept certain doctrinaire beliefs (as when, for instance, one subscribes to Marx's theory of history), and it is precisely against the doctrinaire that formalism works so powerfully. For it is with religious or political beliefs as it was with the ghost in *Hamlet:* if as monotheists we object that polytheism is an illusion or falsehood, we cannot read the *Iliad* or the *Odyssey,* worlds where the Olympian deities are as real as sun and rain; if as atheists or agnostics we cannot believe in any godhead at all, the *Divine Comedy* and *Paradise Lost* become inaccessible. The formalist claim to immanence thus rests on the deeper principle that when we are inside *Hamlet* we do believe in ghosts, and that when we are inside *Paradise Lost* we do believe in God and Satan and the angels, and that this always involves an absolute suspension of external systems of belief—especially those that, like Marxism, purport to give an exhaustive and exclusive account of reality.

Though he is profoundly sympathetic to the claim that New Criticism represented a form of escapism, then, Jameson understands the need to attack it on altogether different grounds. This he does through the assertion that formalism, for all those claims to immanence that have seemed so persuasively to checkmate the objections of any "political" approach, is really a form of transcendent interpretation in disguise. In the name of a "humanism" that operates by universalizing the system of bourgeois social relations under capitalism into an idea of "humanity" existing outside of historical time, that is, formalist criticism simply rewrites literary works in terms of an ethical master code that is a product of its historical moment. What Jameson calls the weak ethical rewritings of the New Criticism are then offered as a kind of wisdom about a "permanent human condition" that does not exist except as a mirage projected by formalism itself. Thus New Criticism dwells eternally in an airy castle of its own construction.

This is, on the face of it, a surprising charge, not least because the claims of formalist criticism to immanence would seem to deny the sort of allegorizing Jameson perceives here; it is no more obvious that the interpretation actually produced by the New Criticism is "ethical" than that it is "Freudian" or "Marxist" or whatever. And this remains true when we compare New Criticism with critical approaches that are openly ethical in Jameson's sense: Matthew Arnold's *The*

Function of Criticism, for instance, written out of the deep Victorian moral anxiety that would lead Arnold to seek a kind of social salvation in literature, or Leavis's *The Great Tradition* and the criticism of the *Scrutiny* group, which was the direct continuation of Arnold's project. Yet it is not clear that ethical criticism of this sort is *interpretation* at all, which is doubtless what led Northrop Frye in the *Anatomy of Criticism,* the *Summa* of the formalist program, to renounce evaluation or "taste criticism" as the end of literary study.

Jameson's response to this objection is subtle and resourceful: we do not see the ethical "master code" in the name of which New Criticism allegorized literature, he argues, because we share with that criticism an ideological climate in which it does not look like a "doctrine" as such. It is the idea of an integrated identity, a whole self, a stable and balanced individual psyche, that is the master code of New Critical practice, and if it does not appear as such to us it is because we accept its categories (the self, the individual psyche, etc.) as universal categories of human nature. Though Jameson does not say so, there is a clear implication that this idea is an ideological reverse image of the estranged and alienated and fragmented reality that is modern life under capitalism. So the claims of formalist criticism to immanence must be rejected on the double grounds that formalism operates through a disguised transcendence and that it is transparently ideological in the old "bad" sense of perpetuating an oppressive social system.

The apparent ease with which Jameson is able to "unmask" formalism as transcendent interpretation, moreover, strongly suggests that he would be able to do the same with any interpretive mode making claims to immanence (as he has indeed done in various articles, "unmasking" structuralism, for instance, as transcendent interpretation using as its master code Language itself). Even as he has seemed to borrow from Deleuze and Guattari an instrument for bringing to light any hidden master code or master narrative, that is, there is the implication that the instrument could as easily be turned against them. Jameson's underlying claim here, which he is content to leave undeveloped, is that the master code of any interpretive method is the ideology it works to perpetuate. Since all methods are ultimately ideological, all interpretation will thus necessarily be transcendent, and immanence as Deleuze and Guattari demand it a mirage. Is the only choice, then, between reductivism and silence?

There is no simple escape from the dilemma. The possibility of escape lies, Jameson will argue, not in any attempt to abolish transcendent interpretation as such, but in pursuing interpretation through rising orders of generality in such a way that successive master codes or master narratives are transformed into the steps of an ascent to a view of the social totality. This is the interpretive system, in short, which Jameson means to be the main contribution of *The Political Unconscious,* and it is the system that will occupy us in this and the next chapter. For the present, we need only be aware that this is the system by which Jameson will take us in ascending stages from the individual literary work to a view of History and Necessity, and that we shall see at each stage that the previous one was merely temporary or provisional.

Like Wittgenstein at the end of the *Tractatus,* that is, telling the reader that all his previous propositions are nonsensical, a ladder that must be kicked away now that the ascent has been made, Jameson rests his theory of interpretation on a certain notion of *necessary* error that in one sense is very old but in another violates commonsensical notions of error. For common sense tells us that truth provides a vantage point from which we see that error was unnecessary, as, looking at a map after having lost our way to someone's house, we see that we could have eliminated an hour of confused wandering about and come there directly. Yet the alternative view is as old at least as Plato, and particularly evident in those neoplatonic systems that insist that one must begin from the imperfections of this world to reach the ideality of the other. In Marxist terms, the ascent involves that idea we have already seen Jameson to share with Althusser—namely, the idea of ideology not simply as error but as functional or necessary error. Thus ideology becomes in Jameson's system the means of transcending the merely ideological.

Jameson will discover the precursor of his own system of interpretation, in turn, in the unlikeliest of places: in that great system of patristic and medieval exegesis the aim of which was, as he says, to rewrite the scriptural inheritance of the Jews into a form usable by Gentiles. Here again, as with his earlier "historicizing" of the Freudian model of interpretation, Jameson's aim is to dispose of the historically determined and merely contingent "content" of an interpretive system and leave the system itself intact for his own dialectical use. As Aristotle glimpsed behind a wilderness of particular arguments that fixed world of universally valid forms out of which he made syllogistic logic, Jameson is able to glimpse behind systems as widely separated as patristic exegesis and Freudian psychoanalysis forms that, invested with the new content of dialectical interpretation, may be put to powerful use.

Since Jameson's account of the medieval system is characteristically compressed, and since it nonetheless contains the most important key to his system of interpretation, we will do well to follow the steps of his analysis closely. The four levels of medieval exegesis, we recall, are the literal, allegorical, moral, and anagogical. They may be represented as follows:

ANAGOGICAL (Mankind: the "collective" level)

$\uparrow$

MORAL (The individual: the "psychological" level)

$\uparrow$

ALLEGORICAL (Christ: the "interpretive code")

$\uparrow$

LITERAL (Israel: actual history)

Jameson's points about this system will be: (1) that in the medieval scheme each level *generates* the next as a new or further level of meaning, and (2) that it does so through *allegory* conceived as *ideological investment*, in Althusser's sense of ideology as the ways in which men imagine their relationship to the "transpersonal" categories of society and history.

At the literal level, then, we have what appears to be merely a historical record: the story of the Jews in their kingdoms and their wanderings, the record of a Semitic people moving within the narrow limits of time and geography through various vicissitudes as a national or tribal group. The complex reality that stands here to be impoverished, as Deleuze and Guattari have it, by any attempt to allegorize it in terms of a master narrative is of course not the Old Testament itself but the historical "referent," the actual historical experience, to which the Old Testament corresponds as document or record. The way in which this record generates another level of meaning, however, is clear enough: in the Old Testament history is God's book, and actual historical events are *already* symbolic, already available as types or figures of some truth lying beyond their own literal status as mere occurrences or events.

If we have the objections of Deleuze and Guattari in mind, however, it is the next level, the allegorical, that very obviously contains the threat of impoverishment, for this is the level at which the events of Christ's life as recounted in the Gospels are taken to supply the "meaning" of events in the Old Testament. Thus, to take the standard exegetical example cited by Jameson, Christ's redemption of mankind in the New Testament is taken to fulfill the promise implicit in God's deliverance of his people out of Egypt in the Old, the Egyptian bondage of Israel being a type or prefiguration of the bondage to sin from which the sacrifice of Christ delivered mankind. All the requirements Deleuze and Guattari had in mind seem to be met here: the life of Christ is obviously being used as a "master narrative" in their sense, and the multitudinous events of Old Testament history are being reduced to events in the life of one individual. Is the medieval allegorical level, then, inevitably an impoverishment of the literal or historical level?

Obviously not. As Jameson observes, allegory is an impoverishment only when it insists on a one-to-one equivalence between interpretation and text, as when the Greeks, embarrassed in their "rational" stage by Homer's polytheism, reinterpreted the quarrels of the Homeric gods as conflicts between abstract vices and virtues. What Deleuze and Guattari have not seen is that interpretation reduces or impoverishes only when it operates in the name of some false or limiting category, as Freudian psychoanalysis impoverishes by allegorizing lived experience in the name of the individual psyche. The allegorical level of medieval exegesis does not impoverish in this way because the "individual" to whose life story it "reduces" Old Testament history is not an individual in the ordinary sense but Christ, God Himself become man and, as God, containing mankind within Himself. Thus the allegorical level does not—indeed, cannot—stop with itself but immediately generates a third level of meaning.

It is the third, or moral, level of interpretation, then, that impoverishment or reductiveness seems most clearly to threaten, for this is the level at which everything is reformulated in terms of the ordinary individual. To pursue the example we have chosen, it is here that the story of Christ's death and resurrection is reinterpreted on the "psychological" level as the individual's bondage to sin and his or her release through Christ's sacrifice into a world of grace and redemption. Yet here, once again, there can be no real "reduction to the individual," for in his relation to Christ the individual represents mankind as a whole, is within himself or herself that entire humanity for whose sake, rather than for the sake of this sinner or that, Christ died upon the cross. So again interpretation cannot stop short at this level, but generates yet another level of meaning to which it must then ascend.

Interpretation does cease at this fourth, or anagogic, level, at which the story of the individual is reinterpreted as the collective story of mankind in history, born in bondage to original sin, saved by Christ's sacrifice, and reborn ("delivered out of Egypt" in a transcendent sense) into that divine and eternal order that will come into existence at the end of the world. The essential point is that interpretation may cease at this level because interpretation is something mankind has need of only *inside* history, in that imperfect world where the mind sees as through a glass darkly, and that with the abolition of History as such—that apocalypse just glimpsed at this last level—interpretation as a human activity becomes needless. Thus interpretation becomes, in the system of the Church fathers, a means of ascending from the dusty wanderings of the Jews to a vision of the collective destiny of humankind.

Though the medieval system will remain the direct inspiration for Jameson's system of interpretation, as we shall see in the next chapter, he does not move directly from it to his own system, but first pauses to examine in detail the archetypal system of Northrop Frye. The greatness of Frye as a modern critic, in Jameson's eyes, is that in an era of formal analysis he has refused to neglect the social and historical dimension of literature, to the point that his criticism may be read as a meditation on the destiny of the human community. Indeed, as Jameson points out, Frye may be viewed as having reinvented in modern terms the medieval system of exegesis, and thus as having embodied in his criticism the virtues of religious thought as (in the somewhat "heretical" terms that Jameson, with the courage of an unorthodox Marxism, takes from Durkheim) the space in which the community thinks through its destiny.

Jameson's discussion of Frye is detailed and acute, but enough has been said about the central issues involved to warrant a compressed summary here. In essence, says Jameson, what Frye has done is reinvent the four levels of medieval exegesis but in such a way as to *reverse* the last two levels in their relation to each other so as to short-circuit the meditation on collective destiny he has begun. Frye's third level, that is, becomes in his system the level of collective destiny, and his fourth a level of purely individual revelation; thus Frye becomes, because of the ideological limitations imposed on him, an unwitting promulgator of that "ideology of desire" of which one heard so much during the countercultural years of the 1960s, an ideology of merely personal or individual ecstasy in place of that collective transformation of social reality which is the apocalypse of Marxist thought.

The specific way in which this comes about can be briefly sketched. As every reader of Frye's *Anatomy of Criticism* will recall (the same scheme is presented even more attractively and accessibly in *The Educated Imagination,* in which Frye outlines his system for a general public), his third level or "phase" of interpretation is the archetypal, at which we encounter the city, the garden, the sheepfold, and so on as permanent forms or archetypes of the imagination. How they come to function this way is explained in Frye's larger system, in which human desire is seen as the driving energy or force in human civilization, and civilization itself as the world men create out of nature as an alien environment. Literature, with its ideal cities and gardens, is in this context the imaginative expression of the goal of work, work being the means through which nature is transformed into civilization.

Frye's fourth and final level or "phase," then, becomes the anagogic, but this is not that anagogical level at which medieval exegesis read the outlines of the collective story of mankind. The anagogic is for Frye the level at which the imagination outstrips the forms of its desire (the gardens and cities and sheepfolds of the third level) and comes to perceive the entire universe as something contained within the mind of man. The origins of Frye's system in his first great critical book on Blake's poetry are overpoweringly evident here, and Jameson is right to stress the sense in which this is a vision of the universe as the throbbing libidinal body of some apocalyptic Blakean man, a recontainment of the collective energies of mankind within the limits of some merely personal ecstasy. Frye's expansion of the individual mind to the point that it imaginatively contains the universe thus fails to burst through the ideological limitations of the category of individuality itself.

Frye's recontainment of potentially revolutionary collective energies, then, those volcanic energies that when they have long enough been bottled up by social and political oppression will erupt to transform the world, is due to his own repression of History, his need to confine for the time being within conceptual boundaries what will not, when the time comes, be subject to confinement on any terms whatever. Frye's genius was to see that interpretation that is to escape the objections raised by Deleuze and Guattari, the nietzschean charge of reductiveness and impoverishment, must ascend beyond mere local allegory to a larger vision of human community; his failure, inevitable given his ideological situation, was a failure of nerve. The only mode of criticism exempt from ideological limitation, as Jameson means to demonstrate, and thus not threatened by a similar failure of nerve, is Marxist interpretation.

6

The Political Unconscious

Jameson's doctrine of the political unconscious is not, it should be evident by now, a loose or impressionistic attempt to adapt Freudian psychoanalytic theory to the demands of political analysis. What Jameson means by the unconscious, or by the collective denial or repression of underlying historical contradictions by human societies, is perfectly rigorous. Indeed, it is in one sense the point of Jameson's "historicizing" of Freudian theory to demonstrate that Freud himself discovered the political unconscious but, imprisoned through ideological circumstance within such illusory categories as "personal identity," "the individual psyche," and the like, was in no position to understand the consequences of his discovery. The truth of Freudian theory lies in the concept of repression (that is, that there are certain forms of "normal" functioning that can only be explained through a suppression of the intolerable or "abnormal"), and this truth remains available to non- or post-Freudian modes of interpretation.

Jameson's system might seem to be vulnerable to a charge of looseness or vagueness, too, insofar as it invokes the notion of a "collective consciousness" which, in its repression of history, might appear to have the mythopoeic overtones of some inverted Jungianism. Yet here Jameson draws great strength and precision from that body of structuralist thinking that in recent years has demonstrated that the notion of "individual consciousness" is incoherent except as it is already taken to imply some idea of a collective consciousness or total social system, much as "sentence" is incoherent except as we understand it already to presuppose a language or total system of linguistic rules. A baby raised in isolation, we understand, would not be a human being, and an adult going to a desert island takes his society with him; when Aristotle described man as a social animal he had already glimpsed a certain constitutive relation between social systems and their individual units. Jameson's only further point as a Marxist is that separation or individuality *at the level of consciousness itself* is a symptom of estrangement from the life of the collectivity.

Given the same background in structuralist thinking, too, Jameson's notion of narrative as the specific mechanism through which the collective consciousness represses historical contradictions is both rigorous and precise. For what I have called the narratological claim behind Jameson's treatment of actual narratives, the idea that narrative as an epistemological category is the contentless form of our most basic experience of reality, inescapably ascribes to narrative a collective function. To imagine a story, if we may paraphrase Wittgenstein as Jameson invokes him at one point, is to imagine the society within which it is told. Jameson's contribution here rests on the insight that narrative is always a part of the "normal" functioning of a society—that is, narrative belongs to everyday life as lived on the social surface—and at the same time has something "abnormal" about it as repressing an intolerable reality beneath (the same doubleness that slips, jokes, dreams, etc., had for Freud).

The crucial question remaining about the doctrine of the political unconscious, then, does not concern the elements of Jameson's system (the mechanism of collective repression and its workings) but the question of repression itself. What is there in the political unconscious, in short, that makes it the collective equivalent of that lawless realm of repressed instinctuality that is the Freudian unconscious? Jameson's use of the standard term "contradiction" is not much help here, especially as it traces to Marx's own borrowing from Hegel. For contradiction in Hegel, it will be recalled, is mainly a dynamic concept, a principle of the unfolding of reality: an egg is "contradictory" with itself insofar as it already contains the not-egg or negation-of-egg (the Hegelian or dialectical chicken) it will become when hatched, thus demonstrating an underlying reality that is identifiable with neither egg nor chicken but with the process of which each is a separate manifestation.

So far as Marx simply took over this concept and applied it within his own historical scheme to the systems of socioeconomic relations he called modes of production, the term remains not only intelligible but elegant. On this view, relations of production develop within a society as one of the efficient means of material production; roughly speaking, they are that system of legal and property arrangements which most efficiently allows a society to exploit its relation with the material environment. Contradiction, on this view (which is Marx's view in, for instance, the *Contribution to the Critique of Political Economy*) is what occurs when the underlying forces of material production begin to outstrip the system of social relations to which they earlier gave rise, much as a crustacean, having excreted one exoskeleton for its use, sheds it and grows another. This is the sense in which, to use the Hegelian metaphor favored by classical Marxism, bourgeois society matured in the womb of feudalism, leading to the social revolution through which the bourgeois order came to supplant feudal relations.

We glimpse here, perhaps, the moment at which contradiction begins to imply a source of revolutionary impulses (and we do well to recall now that the proletarian revolution was for Marx merely the last in a succession of revolutions) and may therefore legitimately become, in Jameson's system, the social and political equivalent of that seething sphere of repressed instinctuality that is Freud's unconscious. The question of what is repressed, then, may be answered in obvious terms: it is revolution itself, the "glorious Phantom" of Shelley's "England in 1819," the grim Spectre that stalks Europe in *The Communist Manifesto,* shoved down by a tremendous effort of the collective consciousness beneath the surface of "normal" social relations and kept there for the time being. Here we have one powerful reason why Jameson repeatedly invokes Althusser's notion of History as an "absent cause": in any moment of history in which social cataclysm does not take place there is only, so to speak, the "not-revolution" that has never occurred. So what is visible, there for interpretation, is the way the ideological structure registers the strain of having kept it repressed.

Yet none of this answers the question of why the contents of the political unconscious should in literal terms be intolerable to the collective consciousness, and Jameson does no more than hint at an answer. There are, I think, two, the first being that, to invoke our own historical moment as an example, the real notion of a proletarian revolution involves not some minor adjustment of social relations but a conflagration of forms, of modes of being, of individuality and experience *as such* so total as to be literally unimaginable to the bourgeois mind. The bourgeois fears mob violence, rape, the clubbing to death of his children, the rampage through the museum—it is a spiritual death for the bourgeois intellectual to imagine a Brueghel or a Rembrandt being thrown on the bonfire, a world in which no one will ever view a Raphael again—and yet these are only the dim figures of a revolution in which bourgeois consciousness itself will become extinct. Though the terror exists only for those caught on the wrong side of History, these comprise Jameson's present audience. It is no wonder he treads lightly here.

The threat of proletarian revolution as repressed by bourgeois consciousness is the intolerable viewed so to speak from above; the same threat viewed from below brings us closer to Jameson's second reason for regarding the contents of the political unconscious as intolerable. For what appears from this nether perspective is exploitation as psychological hell: what the slave knows, what you would know if I stood over you with a gun every day and forced you to grow food for my table. For Jameson as a Marxist this is not, of course, some dark paranoid fantasy: it is the nightmare of history itself as men and women have always lived it, a nightmare that must be repressed as a condition of psychological survival not only by the master but also by the slave, not only by the bourgeoisie but also by the proletariat. The paradox that an oppressed class must be taught to recognize its own real interests is usually explained in Marxism through such notions as ideological hegemony, but for Jameson it is equally due to the fact that denial or repression is, even for the oppressed, a means of survival.

The collective repression of the historical nightmare is a fact so massive, then, so powerful and all inclusive, that Jameson can feel justified in founding upon it a system of literary interpretation that is also a theory of history. Here too is the justification of Jameson's method of "semantic reconstruction," in its affinities with Foucauldian or Nietzschean "genealogy," through which he will elicit from the structure of a cultural text that unexpressed subtext or *hors texte* it cannot acknowledge. For collective repression only gives us, once again, what did *not* happen, the "not-revolution" whose presence is revealed in the traces of an impinging pressure from beneath on the ideological structures of a society. Like an aerospace engineer reconstructing from isolated bits of twisted metal a story of tremendous pressures of stress and temperature, Jameson reading a novel by Balzac or Conrad is giving an account less of a visible structure than of an absent cause.

How, then, does a general insight into the nature of collective repression translate into the actual interpretation of narrative? Though his discussions of particular texts offer the richest and most suggestive answer to this question, Jameson offers as a preliminary methodological parable a moment of anthropological analysis by Claude Lévi-Strauss. The great advantage of the example is that it shows, still within a relatively simple context, how Jameson's method is to work, but it has the further advantage of showing structuralist analysis as deployed by an anthropologist inspired by Marxism, thus at once reflecting Jameson's current indebtedness to structuralist thought and foreshadowing the dynamic or dialectical use to which he will put his similar analyses. Lévi-Strauss's interest is, as Jameson's will be, in the cultural artifact as the symbolic resolution of a real contradiction, an attempt to resolve on an imaginary level the intolerability of a lived dilemma.

The methodological parable Jameson chooses is Lévi-Strauss's treatment of the facial decorations of the Caduveo Indians, which begins in the discovery of a purely formal or aesthetic contradiction: Caduveo decorations are patterns organized along an axis running obliquely to that of the face, so that if one pictures the facial features as a purely formal pattern organized along a vertical axis, there occurs the clash on which Lévi-Strauss bases his analysis. Yet what it means to call this tension between two purely visual patterns a "contradiction," especially as the analysis is going to end by disclosing an underlying contradiction in the Marxist sense, is never clear, and Jameson's discussion does nothing to make it clearer. The point is a crucial one for Jameson's entire system, since it involves the claim that what Lévi-Strauss is doing so far is purely *immanent* analysis, describing the Caduveo decorations in their own formal or visual terms as pattern only.

Lévi-Strauss's predisposition to find a formal or aesthetic contradiction here, that is, may fairly be described as "political" insofar as he has been told what to look for by a Marxist analysis of history, but much still depends on that contradiction's existing in purely objective or structural terms: it must not be, if this truly is immanent analysis, a pattern imposed on the raw visual data by the requirements of Lévi-Strauss's system. And in rough terms one can see what he has in mind here: if a sailor were to have tattooed on his chest an eagle the visual axis of which ran from one shoulder to the opposing hip, it would be curious. If all the sailors in the fleet did this, they might be seen as constituting a society worthy of anthropological inspection. Yet this does not escape the objection that the sailors—or, equally, the Caduveo—simply see this as the appropriate way to do tattoos, and that any notion of "tension" or "clash" or "contradiction" merely reflects the different expectations imported by the outside observer.

The claim to immanent analysis must rest, in short, on the further claim that aesthetic objects project their own norms; this is the context in which we want to say, objectively speaking, that a landscape painting hung upside down has been hung wrong. When the same principle takes the form of an internal tension between elements, as in the distorted skull of Holbein's "The Ambassadors," it thus demands not correction but explanation. The facial decorations of the Caduveo, then, are something like a series of perfectly ordinary landscapes in which everything except one characteristic object—say, oak trees—has been painted right side up. The fact demands explanation, and it will do no good to explain that this particular tribe has a myth about oak trees, for the myth too will then from a Marxist perspective demand explanation in terms of an underlying contradiction. This will be the basis of Jameson's claim that, at the first level of analysis, he respects the integrity of aesthetic form quite as much as any formalist critic: interpretation that begins in immanent analysis can scarcely be accused of distorting the text to achieve "Marxist" results.

If we grant that Lévi-Strauss's analysis begins in the wholly immanent analysis of a formal contradiction, then, what is the underlying social contradiction of which it is a symbolic resolution? The answer has a specifically Marxist coloration: the Caduveo are a hierarchical society already organized by various relations of domination; there exists, for instance, a hereditary aristocracy, and beyond that women are in a subservient relation to men, younger people to older, and so on. The hierarchical nature of Caduveo society is outwardly represented, moreover, in its division into three separate and endogamous castes. The social restrictions on marriage exchanges and kinship patterns thus translate into the terms of everyday experience the rigidity of hierarchical domination. This is social contradiction as the Caduveo actually live it, and, living it, must attempt to resolve it on some level other than the real.

How might the same contradiction be resolved in social terms? Lévi-Strauss describes by way of example the social structure of the neighboring Guana and Bororo, also organized by relations of domination outwardly reflected in caste systems. But here in both cases the castes are divided into moieties among which there is free marital exchange that, appearing to work in an unrestricted and egalitarian way, masks the real relations of domination underlying the social surface. Thus the Guana and Bororo achieve at the institutional level an apparent resolution of contradiction, one no less illusory in its way than that of the Caduveo but capable of draining off intolerable social tensions before they demand a last outlet at the imaginary or symbolic level. Thus it is that Lévi-Strauss is able to discover in an underlying contradiction the "meaning" of Caduveo facial decorations.

The Caduveo example contains the essence of Jameson's theory and method: like Lévi-Strauss, he will always begin by asking of what real contradiction a given text is an imaginary or symbolic resolution, on a principle that remains meaningful whether the "text" is a pattern of facial decorations, a myth, or a novel produced in industrial Europe. Yet there is not a perfect one-to-one equivalence between Lévi-Strauss's method and Jameson's, for in the Caduveo example everything needed to make the notion of contradiction intelligible is right to hand; this is, after all, the point of Lévi-Strauss's description of caste systems, kinship customs, marriage exchanges, and the rest. Jameson's claim, on the other hand, will be that the contradiction occurs at the level of an invisible or underlying subtext which in one sense is not there.

This brings us to the most complicated moment in Jameson's theory, one that he presents in terms of Kenneth Burke's prior theory of texts as symbolic acts. For, to employ Burke's own stress-shifting technique, the paradoxical fact is that a text is both a symbolic *act* and a *symbolic* act: that is, it is a genuine act in that it tries to do something to the world, and yet it is "merely" symbolic in the sense that it leaves the world untouched. The ambiguity belongs, of course, not just to texts but to symbolic acts generally. If, having gotten into an argument in a bar in the rough part of town, I enforce my contempt for someone else's point by making an obscene gesture (the standard obscene gesture, let us say), my act remains "merely" symbolic in that it stands in harmlessly for my having punched my adversary in the nose. And yet my gesture is a genuine act nonetheless, or there would be no danger, as there palpably is, of getting my own nose punched in return.

This is the point in his theory, in short, where Jameson must deal with the eternally problematic relationship between the text and reality, literature and the world, the symbolic and the Real. And he is aware as he does so that error lies to either side of a middle course: the pitfall of vulgar Marxism, which so stresses the "merely" symbolic status of the text that it renders it bodiless, the passive reflection of an underlying brute reality called base or infrastructure, or the pitfall of structuralism, which so stresses the status of the text as act, and of language itself as having power to organize and constitute the world, that all worlds independent of language disappear. Jameson's course between Scylla and Charybdis is to insist that the text *does* generate its own reality (that is, any reality existing independent of it), but that this reality then is independent or "real." The paradox is thus that a text conjures into existence as its subtext a History that cannot be seen directly, but that was nevertheless there all along.

The claim is neither as paradoxical nor as perverse as it sounds, and in fact if we trouble ourselves to keep in mind Jameson's Freudian model it becomes unextraordinary. For it is the essence of the Freudian unconscious that it cannot possibly be seen directly, but must be viewed, as in *The Interpretation of Dreams,* by way of inference from whatever is visible or analyzable; the unconscious is not there, so to speak, precisely because the dream was successful in keeping it out of sight. For Jameson, the same insight explains the semantic relationship between language and reality. We have a hard time saying what the "world" is that language is supposed to mean by referring to—and the longer structuralism looks at it the more this world appears to be constituted or created by language itself—and yet we tend to look for it nonetheless. Jameson explains both why it is there and why we cannot see it: it is the *unexpressed* reality that underlies all social use of language.

We may glimpse at this point something like the ultimate rationale for reading literary texts, as Lévi-Strauss looked at the facial decorations of the Caduveo, with an eye to their grounding in the contradictions of an unexpressed subtext. For the claim will be, as Jameson says, that the text as symbolic act always entertains an active relationship with the real, that it draws the real into its own texture, but that, and this is the crucial point, it does these things in the simultaneous moment of *denying* the real. So again we arrive, this time from a slightly different direction, at the paradox: when we read a novel with Jameson we are always going to be reconstructing the subtext that it generates as the necessary completion of its meaning, what Jameson would call the "semantic precondition" of its meaning anything, or even being readable at all, and yet at the same time the novel is going to "say" that the subtext is not there.

As Jameson's invocation of Lévi-Strauss and his repeated description of nineteenth-century fiction as the *pensée sauvage* of the bourgeoisie demonstrate, it is examples from magic and ritual that make things clearest here. Suppose, for instance, that we were to see an old peasant woman leave on her doorstep every night a dish of milk, and suppose we know too that she believes no natural creatures (cats, children, etc.) to be abroad after nightfall, so that the act is clearly one of propitiation toward supernatural beings who have the power to do humans harm. The important point is not simply that the act in itself projects the realm of supernatural or magical creatures as really existing (would be meaningless *as* an act without that), but also that the act aims to modify their existence and behavior in a certain way: that is, to appease them so that they will not do the mischief they would otherwise do. Thus we have, in Jameson's terms, not only the *projection* of a subtext but also its *denial* or *negation:* the "meaning" of the old woman's act is the harm or evil that, so long as the magic is successful, never gets expressed.

Magic and ritual provide useful examples, in turn, because they have the virtue of suggesting the sense in which *all* symbolic acts are "magical," what Burke points to in observing that a symbolic act wants to have an impact on the world while leaving the world untouched. The grounding of the act in the contradictions of an unexpressed subtext is not fully brought out, however, in the example of the peasant woman, so let us imagine a slightly more elaborate example, this time vaguely in the spirit of *The Golden Bough:* we know of a tribe that annually chooses a king from among its own number, feasts and pampers him through the summer and autumn and winter months, then slays him in the spring when the seed for that year's crop is put into the ground. The slaying is, let us further suppose, an altar ritual, with chants and prayers for the fertility of the coming harvest. What Jameson means by saying that the Real is inscribed in symbolic acts is evident here, as well as the sense in which it represents, and may be grasped by interpretation as, the imaginary solution of a real contradiction.

The sacrifice of the king is, obviously enough, ambiguous or paradoxical in Burke's sense: on the one hand it is a "merely" symbolic act—we know the amount of moisture in and the fertility of the soil, for example, are not going to be affected, as they would, say, by the genuine acts of irrigating the fields or manuring the ground—and yet on the other we are compelled to recognize it as an *act:* it is unintelligible except as an attempt designed to have an impact or work a change upon the world. Then too we can immediately grasp what Jameson would call a contradiction at the formal or aesthetic level: this is a ritual in which there is an opposing and overwhelming tension between the actual sacrificial event (death, the end of life) and its sacerdotal context (chants and prayers for fertility or renewal of life). The contradiction, moreover, as something written right into the formal structure of the ritual, is available to purely immanent analysis.

The same formal contradiction occurs at another level as well, namely in the fact that this society does not simply take one of its number as the random victim of its annual sacrifice, but goes through the ritual of choosing a king and allowing him a year of domination before he is put to death (we may imagine, if it makes the case more vivid, that the king during his year of rule exercises despotic power, even to the point where he may have others put to death). In such a case, the society would clearly be exploiting the semiotic potential of its own social structure (a "sign system" of "high" and "low" status) to maximize the value of the sacrifice and thus its value as an act of propitiation. Thus again we have a formal paradox—the "highest" member of a society being subjected to the "lowest" fate of an involuntary death—that is accessible to purely formal analysis.

As a symbolic act, then, the sacrifice of the king clearly attempts to resolve at the imaginary level a real contradiction, which in this case is the dominant relation of nature (rainfall and the seasonal cycle, natural calamities like fire or flood, the leaching or salinization of the soil, etc.) to an agricultural society; this is the ultimate "relation of domination" lying behind those relations of domination in the social structure for which the sacrifice of the ruler may now be grasped as an act of atonement. In Marxist terms, then, the underlying contradiction occurs at the submerged or hidden level of Necessity: a mysterious and impersonal force ("nature") here "owns the means of production," and unless it behaves benevolently the tribe will starve; it is the intolerability of this threat that the sacrifice attempts to resolve or negate, and that must thus be reconstructed as the "subtext" of the ritual considered as a "text." Such reconstruction is possible because the ritual-as-text has inscribed within itself the Real.

At the same time, the meaning of History as an absent cause, something outside all ritual or narrative structures whatever, is that the "real contradiction" addressed by the text as a symbolic act is not that ultimate contradiction that in Marxist thought can only be resolved through "collective praxis"—that is, revolution. It is, rather, contradiction as it appears in ideological form, as an aporia or "antinomy" or irresolvable logical bind. In the case of our king sacrifice, for instance, this would doubtless be on the social or agricultural level what Hegel long ago saw as the paradox of sexual reproduction, that sexual consummation is a moment simultaneously of regeneration and of death, for the act that perpetuates the species by begetting new life also inevitably signals the mortality of its individual members. Such antinomies as this of death-in-birth are, for Jameson, what are addressed by such rituals as the tribal sacrifice of a king, such mythological narratives as that of Christian sacrifice, and such individual narratives as epic poems and novels produced within historical societies.

Our discussion of texts as symbolic acts brings us now to the three horizons of Jameson's system of interpretation, within the first horizon of which it has without acknowledgment been taking place. This system is Jameson's answer on the one hand to the crude typologizing of "vulgar Marxist" criticism and on the other to the obviously "ideological" character of systems like medieval scriptural exegesis or Frye's archetypal criticism. I have hinted at the direction and dynamics of its interpretive movement, which is from the "text" in its ordinary sense of an individual work and "history" in the ordinary sense of year-to-year events through three concentric and ever-widening interpretive horizons to a final view of History as, in Jameson's formulation, the ultimate ground and untranscendable horizon of textual meaning. We must conclude our consideration of his program by considering this movement in detail.

As Jameson invokes it, the idea of a "horizon" is borrowed ultimately from classical phenomenology, but more immediately from Gadamer, in whose relativistic account of historical knowledge it serves to enforce the point that no item of knowledge is conceivable except within some ordered and closed structure of knowledge. This is to insist on the now-familiar point that "facts" count as such only against some prior background of hypotheses and beliefs, but also on the point that social and historical as well as scientific knowledge operate this way: to understand witchcraft or a fertility ritual or the "hysteria" of Freud's turn-of-the-century Viennese patients is to move within an alien horizon of thought and perception. A similar notion is sometimes invoked in the philosophy of science: where ordinary men see a tree, we say, the botanist sees a system of respiration and photosynthesis and the physicist a whirling dance of colorless particles. The relation in such instances between horizon—what in general terms we refer to as "ordinary language," "botany," and "physics," respectively—and object is very similar to the one implied by Jameson's system.

Let us suppose, then, that we have read a Balzac novel as a symbolic act resolving in imaginary terms some underlying contradiction. At this first level, our horizon is what ordinary criticism would call the historical context of the novel: Europe after the failure of the French and the Napoleonic revolutions, an emergent industrial economy, the social dominance of the new bourgeoisie, etc. The purely passive sense in which they reflect a complex historical background explains, for instance, Marx's own fascination with Balzac's novels, and Jameson's analysis within this first horizon would seem almost formalistic and therefore non-Marxist except for one thing: as we know, his "formal analysis" will not be mere explication de texte but an attempt to locate aesthetic contradiction as disclosing the presence of an underlying social contradiction. The same social contradiction will then be pursued within the next two horizons of the system.

When he has located the contradiction evident within this first horizon, Jameson passes over into the second, which is the *social order* conceived in the broadest sense. Conceiving it in this way involves, in particular, envisioning the social order as something always constituted by a class struggle between a dominant and a laboring class; it is the controlling antagonism between these two classes that both organizes the social structure and assigns places on the social spectrum to such class fractions (the petty bourgeoisie, for example) as do not participate directly in the struggle. Further, Jameson's system demands that we reconceive the social order at the cultural level in the form of a dialogue between antagonistic *class discourses*, which now become the categories within which a Marxist interpretation will rewrite individual texts.

The notion of a "discourse" here draws in general terms on structuralism and in particular upon Foucault; Jameson's contribution is to resituate the concept within the Marxian context of class struggle. Yet Jameson's second horizon is not defined so much by the simple idea of an antagonistic dialogue between class discourses as by the fact that this dialogue is always made possible by what he calls the unity of a shared code. The example Jameson offers, on which I shall expand in a moment, is that of the English Civil War, where the "antagonistic dialogue" between a hegemonic Anglicanism and a suppressed Puritanism shattered into a vast and discordant heterogeneity of militant sects—Independents, Levellers, Fifth Monarchy Men, etc.—each of which defined its *political* relation to all the others in the *religious* terms of prophecy, biblical interpretation, radical theology, and the like. This is what Jameson means when he says that in England in the 1640s religion operated as the shared code within which was fought out the antagonism between opposing discourses.

The English Civil War illustrates as well several of the key concepts on which Jameson's system is drawing at this point. His description of Anglicanism as a "hegemonic theology," for instance, is on one level simply a shorthand reference to Gramsci's theory of ideological hegemony—that is, that a ruling class establishes dominance not only by controlling the legal system, the prisons, and so on, but also by establishing a climate of thought in which the oppressed classes perpetuate their own oppression by learning the values of their masters. Yet behind Jameson's argument now there also stands the authority of Althusser's more recent theory of "ideological state apparatuses," which argues Gramsci's point at the level of "nonrepressive" institutions such as universities, churches, political parties, and the like. A textbook example would be Anglicanism as a hegemonic theology institutionally embodied in the Church of England.

At the same time, Anglicanism is not strictly reducible to the Church of England as a social or political institution, which helps clarify what is meant by calling it a "discourse." Here, once again, the figure in the immediate background is Foucault, whose general point might be illustrated by considering a modern science like physics as a discourse. What this means, first, is that physics as an abstract order of concepts, rules, problems, etc., has the power to make or constitute people what they are: if I wish to become a physicist I can do so only by internalizing the system of rules and concepts called physics, and then when I "speak as a physicist" it is really this same system of rules and concepts speaking through me. Then, second, the "discourse of physics" has the power to create social and even physical institutions: physics departments, conferences, journals, laboratories, etc., all are *generated by* physics as an abstract conceptual order. Foucault's interest is in the repressive implications of this power, but the very same notion of a discourse also fits Jameson's idea of an antagonistic class dialogue.

Our usual tendency, that is, is to think of seventeenth-century Anglicanism primarily as a state institution—the Church of England as a state religion, with Oxford and Cambridge as its seminaries, its cathedrals and bishoprics embodying a national administrative structure, its parish churches and their vicars an institutional presence reaching into every village and hamlet—and only incidentally as that body of abstract thought or theological discourse represented in sermons, controversial pamphlets, works of systematic theology, university curricula, and the like. Yet the whole point of thinking of Anglicanism as a discourse is to see that a reverse perspective is also possible, that "Anglicanism" as an ideology or hegemonic theology may equally be said to have generated the Church of England as an institution, to have created its flesh-and-blood vicars and bishops and its actual cathedrals and village churches as the outward expression of an inner imperative. This is the sense of "discourse" that Jameson's argument now demands.

Then too, we can conceive of Anglicanism as a *dialogical* discourse, in the sense Jameson borrows from Bakhtin, by viewing it as a response to a repressed oppositional voice (in rough terms, a "discourse of Puritanism"). The value of Bakhtin's point is that it insists on the sense in which speech or discourse must always imply a dialogue; if I overhear a voice in conversation in the next room I make sense of it by supplying the idea of a listener or another voice I cannot hear, and even if it turns out that the speaker is physically alone I will construe his discourse as one-half of an imaginary dialogue. A hegemonic discourse, in fact, has just this character: historically speaking we "hear" only one voice because a hegemonic ideology suppresses or marginalizes all antagonistic class voices, and yet the hegemonic discourse remains locked into a dialogue with the discourse it has suppressed. This is why we must picture Anglicanism, even in the comparative serenity of the period preceding the Civil War, as already dialogical in nature.

The Civil War itself, then, figures as the episode in which the silence imposed on a suppressed Puritan discourse was shattered, when that endlessly complex and dynamic antagonism we organize under the names "Anglican" and "Puritan" erupted on the abstract level into the intellectual war of which Milton's great religiopolitical tracts survive as monumental reminders, on the actual or physical level into bloody civil conflict. Jameson's point is that we can call this suppressed discourse "Puritan" with no great historical distortion because religion was for all parties the shared code within which their differences were fought out. Thus it was, for instance, that the "communism" of the Levellers could not take the form of an atheistic doctrine (a doctrine, say, calling for the end of religious delusions as such) but, on the contrary, presented itself as a purified Christianity. The unity of Jameson's second horizon is thus the unity provided by a single dialogue and a shared code.

What happens to the individual text within this second horizon? Jameson's answer is that it must be reconstituted as a *parole* in relation to the *langue* of its class discourse. On the simplest level, Jameson is merely invoking here the standard Saussurean distinction between *parole* and *langue* in linguistics: *parole* as any individual utterance within a language, as when I say "Good morning" to you on the street, *langue* the total system of linguistic rules that makes individual utterance possible. His point will then be that when we interpret, say, a Balzac novel as the *parole* of a *langue*, the class discourse that is the *langue* is, like its Saussurean counterpart, an abstraction nowhere completely present in any body of texts or utterances and something that must always be reconstructed from partial evidence. His further point is that we must continue to conceive of this process dialogically: the class discourse that functions as a *langue* does so by virtue of an antagonistic relation to an opposing discourse.

In practical terms, this means that we complete our view of Jameson's second horizon not simply by reconstructing the *parole-langue* relationship between individual text and class discourse but by then going on to reconstruct the antagonistic class dialogue in which both figure. Jameson cites as examples Ernst Bloch's treatment of the fairy tale as a subversion or "deconstruction" of the aristocratic form of the epic and Eugene Genovese's analysis of black religion as having emptied the content of the slave owners' Christianity while retaining its forms for oppositional or subversive purposes. A similar dynamic is laudably at work, in Jameson's view, in the contemporary reclamation of such marginalized voices as minority, gay, and women's literature, his only caveat as a Marxist being that criticism must be alert to the ways a hegemonic ideology ceaselessly co-opts or reabsorbs or "universalizes" such oppositional voices, thus perpetuating the illusion that there is only a single genuine culture.

Within this second horizon of interpretation, the object of study becomes what Jameson calls the "ideologeme," a kind of minimal unit around which a class discourse is organized. Ultimately, of course, this draws on the notion of the phoneme in linguistics as the minimal phonological unit that creates a word or changes its meaning, as the sound represented by *p* changes *bad* into *pad*. Yet this notion of a "least significant unit" has been expanded in recent years to serve other purposes, as in Foucault's notion of the *épisteme* as a sort of structural equivalent of the Zeitgeist, and Jameson's positing of ideologemes participates in this expansion. The concept is not, one supposes, meant to be rigorous or precise in the way that "phoneme" is rigorous and precise, but simply to make it clear that the ideological structure of class discourses is analyzable *as* a structure; it is to this end that the notion of a "minimal" (rather than a "least significant") unit contributes.

As a minimal unit, the ideologeme can be developed in either of two contrary directions: the conceptual, in which case it appears in rudimentary form as a "pseudo-idea" (opinion, belief, prejudice, etc.) but can then be taken to the length of a complete philosophical system, or the narrative, in which case it appears first as a "protonarrative" (fantasy, anecdote, tale, etc.) but may then be taken to the length of a cultural narrative like a novel or epic poem. Here Jameson's argument draws on a notion of "deep structure" that once again comes from linguistics, this time from the insight of transformational grammar that such sentences as "John ate the apple" and "The apple was eaten by John" point, for all their apparent dissimilarity at the surface level of syntax, to an identical core or kernal sentence at the level of deep structure. In the same way, Nietzsche's philosophy and the novels of Gissing represent, for Jameson, complex transformations worked on the same "core unit" (the idea or "theory" of *ressentiment*) which is their shared ideologeme.

Even within the corpus of Nietzsche's writings, however, we can trace the ways in which *ressentiment* as an ideologeme undergoes both a conceptual and a narrative development. On the conceptual or philosophical level this gives us Nietzsche's "unmasking" of Christian charity as the subversion of a race of masters, strong and self-sufficient in their vitality, by a weak and self-hating race of slaves. On such a reading all ethics then becomes the imposition by the weak of an emasculating ethic on the strong, a ruse through which the masters are themselves infected with a slave mentality. Yet Nietzsche also gives his "theory" of *ressentiment* a narrative form, as the story of Christianity as a slave religion that emerges in the Roman world ultimately to emasculate and bring under its despicable domination the natural masters of society; in the background there then is the "story" of the entire Judeo-Christian tradition as a slave revolt that, too pusillanimous to assert itself at the healthy or Spartacist level of physical violence, is achieved at the level of ethics. Thus *ressentiment* figures as the ideologeme of Nietzschean philosophy and Nietzschean fable alike.

In a general sense it is clear from a Marxist perspective that Nietzsche's notion of *ressentiment* must be ideological: as a philosophy produced within a newly hegemonic capitalism it could be no other. Yet its ideological nature becomes clearest, for Jameson, when *ressentiment* is invoked by a nineteenth-century bourgeoisie and its intelligentsia as the mindless and destructive envy that the have-nots of society always and universally feel toward the haves, thus utterly denying the origins in economic exploitation of all discontent from below, of Peterloo and Chartism and the Paris commune. Add one more modification, the *ressentiment* of failed intellectuals —bad poets, hack journalists, unilluminated philosophers, all the "aesthetic priests" of Nietzsche's system—who then turn against society and we have, Jameson argues persuasively, not only the theme of the alienated intellectual in Gissing's novels but also the coming to light of *ressentiment* as the shared ideologeme of Nietzsche and Gissing.

To bring to light an ideologeme in this manner is to pass over into the third and last horizon of Jameson's system, the horizon of history conceived in the broadest possible sense, as it embraces mankind from its emergence to its eventual extinction as a species. Our earlier discussion perhaps makes clear the danger lurking here: even to speak of history as extending "from X to . . . Y" is to impose a narrative framework on the raw data, in effect to promise to tell a story. And should Jameson as a Marxist critic fulfill this promise in any unqualified way, he will immediately become susceptible to the sort of objection we have already heard powerfully urged by Deleuze and Guattari—that is, that he is merely setting up a "master narrative" or "master code" in terms of which to rewrite literary works, which rewriting or allegorizing will then be exhibited as the underlying "meaning" exposed by a Marxist interpretation.

Jameson is wholly alert to this danger, and he is at his most resourceful in avoiding it. He begins by confronting the concept that most directly leads to the error castigated by Deleuze and Guattari, the notion of a *mode of production* as one of the successive economic "stages" through which mankind has moved from tribal society to capitalism (and will move, after an intermediate stage of socialism, toward communism proper and the withering away of the state). Here the "story" being told is clear—it is Marx's own story of a movement from the tribe to the *gens* and then to the slaveholding society of the *polis* (the "ancient mode of production") and finally to the modes of production embodied in feudalism and capitalism respectively*—as is the process through which Marxist interpretation compels texts to yield up their allegorical meaning according to this story. Here, as we have seen, we encounter Caudwell's pigeonholing of literary works and Goldmann's homologies and even Lukacs's expressive causality—everything, in short, to which Althusser objected in the name of overdetermination and History as an "absent cause."

Given such powerful objections to the standard story of successive modes of production, does the concept retain any value at all? Jameson's answer is yes, and to see why we need only think back to his example of the English Civil War. We have focused so far on the shattering or fragmentation which in the 1640s broke England into a multitude of warring sects and parties, but what Jameson wants us now to see is that such fragmentation *simultaneously* implies an underlying social unity. When we hear two people arguing violently, for in-

---

*Jameson includes the so-called "Oriental mode of production" in his summary account, but its status is a hotly debated issue in contemporary Marxist theory.

stance, it is easy to forget that such disagreement is made possible only by a shared language and a common set of assumptions: should one person speak only Norwegian and the other only Chinese, no argument would be possible in the first place. To observe that religion was the shared code within which parties in the English Civil War fought out their conflicts, then, is similarly to stress an underlying unity.

In this view, which is Jameson's, what the concept of a mode of production is ultimately "about" is not some story of successive economic stages but the possibility of seeing all the social phenomena within a given historical framework as being related to one another as to a totality. In *Capital*, Jameson reminds us, Marx was not trying to give an account of human history but to construct a systematic account of capitalism; the "story" of successive modes of production is thus heuristic merely, and the value of the concept lies in its use as an instrument of social analysis. A mode of production is not, in short, anything we should expect to find in a historically existing society, but a conceptual category that becomes indispensable when we set out to analyze the complex structures of actual historical societies.

If we may not envision them as modes of production, however, what becomes of actual historical societies? The answer, which is central not only to Jameson's third horizon but also to his system as a whole, lies in the concept of *Ungleichzeitigkeit* or the "nonsynchronous development" of the various levels constituting a social whole. The term as Jameson invokes it here is taken from Ernst Bloch, but the concept as it now exerts its force within contemporary Marxism goes back once again to Althusser's notion of overdetermination, especially as it insisted on the relative autonomy of the various levels of the superstructure. This is to insist, for instance, not only that, say, a legal system and a religious system represent within their society separate and relatively autonomous cultural "levels," but that each has a history or temporal development internal to itself and independent of the other. Indeed, this is for Althusser one of the conditions of their relative autonomy.

The process of nonsynchronous social development may be illustrated, as we earlier had occasion to illustrate the concept of overdetermination, by an analogy with the human body. The cells of our bodies, we are informed, replace themselves in a constant process, so constant that at intervals (about every seven years) all the cells in our body are new. But within this total process cells replace themselves at much different rates, skin cells renewing themselves more quickly, for instance, than the cells of the liver or the bones. This is the context in which it makes sense to speak of my body's having a "history of the liver" independent of its "history of the skin"—although, on the principle of overdetermination, both liver and skin are elements of a total system every element of which must be operating: heart beating, lungs respiring, kidneys detoxifying, etc.—to ensure the simultaneous function of every other. Instead of using so clumsy a phrase as "history of the liver," though, one might simply choose to say that liver and skin have in terms of their cellular transformation a nonsynchronous development.

To describe actual historical societies as they appear in this aspect, Jameson borrows from Nicos Poulantzas a term that has gained wide currency in contemporary Marxism: *social formation.* To view a society as a social formation is to see it as a complex structure within which various modes of production coexist and interact. Thus we should expect modern industrial society, for instance, to consist of certain cultural levels—commodity reification would be, for Marxism, the prime example—that trace their inner development back no further than the Industrial Revolution, others incorporating a development from the feudal stage on, others still from tribal society, and all these levels simultaneously interacting with one another to produce the complex dynamic of a society going through the process of historical change. To view societies in this way is to attain what Jameson calls a "metasynchronic" perspective that allows for an account at once of society-as-system and of history as a process of development.

The consequences of this view for a theory of the text are, as we shall see shortly, enormous, but as always for Jameson they are only as important as their political implications. Thus, for instance, the notion of nonsynchronous social development allows him to reconcile the claims of Marxism and radical feminism, which has in recent years urged against any analysis of history in terms of class struggle the cogent claim that in the past women of *all* social classes have been oppressed by men. To view societies as social formations, however, is precisely to expect that earlier levels will coexist with later; in this case, male domination is to be viewed as the virulent cultural survival of a relation developed within tribal society as the earliest human social stage and today coexisting with other, more recent, levels such as commodity reification. The point of the revolution envisioned by Marxism is then that it will abolish all such relations of domination simultaneously.

The third horizon of Jameson's system is thus not history merely but history viewed in this new metasynchronic perspective, to which Jameson gives the name *cultural revolution*. Here a caveat is in order: though "cultural revolution" was suggested to Jameson by events in China in the late 1960s, and though he obviously considers these associations important to his argument, most readers of his book will be confused if they try to make sense of the term by placing it against its background in recent Chinese experience. It is better, for purposes of understanding Jameson, simply to treat the term as one he has made up to describe his third horizon in this new aspect, with "cultural" signalling the sense in which a social formation must be grasped as a total structure or system, "revolution" the sense in which a dynamic of opposing tensions organizes the structure and produces its transformations.

The aim of viewing human history under the aspect of cultural revolution, in short, is to preserve the value of Marx's concept of modes of production without being led by it into the error of vulgar typologizing. We must thus retain the notion of history as change or process (the world after all *is* different now from what it was in the stone age) but also recognize that this is no orderly march from one mode of production to the next but a more complex process of change from one social formation to another in which a new *dominant* emerges but earlier and future strata also coexist (there still are stone age societies in our world). Jameson's examples are the Industrial Revolution and the French Revolution, neither of which was a punctual event but both of which mark the more gradual and problematic process of "transition" in which the social relations of a feudal order gave way to the bourgeois ascendancy under capitalism. Jameson means the term "cultural revolution" to apply to this whole process.

At the same time, the fact that we cannot assign a punctual moment to such transitions means that they represent, to use Jameson's own metaphor, the passage to the surface of a structural antagonism or permanent struggle between the various modes of production coexisting within a given social formation. To use the vocabulary now current, the diachronic thus becomes the manifestation in time of the synchronic: "transition" simply makes visible a structural antagonism that has been there all along, just as dynamic events like the French Revolution, the stuff of ordinary history, demand explanation in the "static" terms of structural tension or opposition. In the same way, a geologist might explain an earthquake as the visible effect of a system or structure of stresses among faults, folds, and the like. So "cultural revolution" is meant to subsume the diachronic and the synchronic, and to posit history as the vast and unnameable horizon about which we use these limited and reductive means of talking.

In a certain sense, the horizon of cultural revolution implies in Jameson's system the end of literary interpretation as such, for this third and last horizon is not just another context within which literary works are to be read; it is, as Jameson puts it, the context within which they know intelligibility. This sounds, on the face of it, like a grandiose claim: does he mean to assert that outside this third horizon a Shakespeare sonnet or a Balzac novel would suddenly turn into meaningless black marks on the page? The answer is that he does, but that the claim is nowhere as grandiose as it sounds, for what Jameson wants us to do is look beyond the local confrontation between reader and text to the common linguistic and cultural codes that make both text and reading a possibility. This is an idea that structuralism has made familiar enough in recent years, and Jameson's claim amounts, really, to nothing more radical than redefining it in terms of class struggle and cultural revolution.

On this view, then, the ultimate context of reading, of the rudimentary act of transforming marks on a page into coherent meanings, is the grand vision of society as structurally co-existing modes of production in antagonistic relation to one another, some left over from earlier stages and dependent now on a new structural dominant—for us, the capitalist market system and its cultural emanations—others anticipating a new or emergent social order for which they have not yet generated space. Jameson's claim is thus on one unextraordinary level that the context of reading or intelligibility is society itself, on an immensely more suggestive level that society must however be seen as a dynamic, heterogeneous system of mutually antagonistic cultural levels. Thus it is that the literary work, what Jameson, making a point, will usually call the "cultural text," mirrors this system and its internal antagonisms.

Once again, this is a theory of the text made familiar in recent years by structuralism and poststructuralism, from which we have gotten the notion of literary works as being composed of heterogeneous orders of discourse each of which may subvert the values, logic, and mimetic claims of the others. Jameson's object is thus to move beyond and subsume such textual theories, and by implication to subsume post-structuralism itself, by showing that no theory of textual heterogeneity is wholly intelligible except as it projects and completes itself in a notion of social or cultural heterogeneity outside the text. Thus the heterogeneous text of poststructuralism becomes, within Jameson's third horizon, an object crisscrossed and intersected by separate sign systems that are themselves cultural manifestations or traces of various structurally coexisting modes of production. Thus poststructuralist theory is recontained within an expanded Marxism.

The object of study within this third horizon then becomes not the heterogeneous text merely, but that text viewed under the aspect of what Jameson calls *the ideology of form,* in which its various registers and discourses reveal to interpretation their "content of form." The phrase, which Jameson borrows from Hjelmslev, is paradoxical only so long as one is imprisoned within an expressive theory of form and content; there is no paradox when we think of forms, as Jameson means us to, as transmitting ideological signals in their own right, as, for instance, the very notion of "epic" as a form or genre also signals, on one level, a notion of heroic values or the heroic world, on another the stage of human economic and social development for which those values served as a hegemonic ideology. When we encounter the epic as a "comically" discordant tone or register in a work like *The Rape of the Lock* or *Tom Jones,* then, we may immediately recognize the sort of heterogeneity Jameson will explain in terms of the ideology of form.

The social resonances of this notion are made clearest, curiously enough, by an example Jameson draws not from literary but from musical form. The "ideological content" of a form like the folk dance, for instance, will be its association with the rhythms and rituals and values of the agricultural society in which it was produced, and it continues to transmit the signals of its ideological content when it is transformed into an aristocratic form like the minuet—indeed, it must, or the whole point of the minuet as aristocrats "playing peasant" would be lost. The same folk dance as a theme in a Romantic symphony then carries with it the history of these earlier transformations in signalling, now, a new ideology, an emergent nationalism that carries within itself, as the symphony carries folk dance and minuet,.the cultural traces of earlier feudal and agrarian orders. The literary equivalent of this heterogeneity of symphonic form is what Jameson will discuss under the name of generic discontinuity.

This brings us to the outer limits of Jameson's interpretive system. Beyond them lie the issues of actual interpretation as pursued by the most original and resourceful Marxist critic now writing, moment after moment of the dialectical shock generated by his brilliant readings of individual texts and authors. Yet to end by considering Jameson a literary critic would be to mistake him and the ultimate purpose of his system, which is to employ the normal categories of literary or cultural study only as a means of transcending them, to move through readings and discussions and analyses only to emerge, on the other side, into a space where one may trace the lineaments of History and Necessity within the social firmament of men and women. To do this is to achieve a revolution within consciousness, the undeniable premonition of that outward revolution toward which the broad stream of an otherwise inscrutable history is carrying the world.

Bibliographical Note

The most useful bibliography of Marxism for the nonspe-
cialist is Terrell Carver's "Guide to Further Reading," ap-
pended to the fourth edition of Isaiah Berlin's classic *Karl
Marx* (New York: Oxford University Press, 1978); this lists
English translations of Althusser's major works. Readers with
a specific interest in Marxism and literature will want to con-
sult Chris Bullock and David Peck, *Guide to Marxist Literary
Criticism* (Bloomington: Indiana University Press, 1980).
Aside from its general thoughtfulness, Terry Eagleton's *Criticism and Ideology* (London: New Left Books, 1976) is valuable
as registering the impact of Althusser on Marxist criticism in
Britain. The single best attempt to situate Marxism in relation
to contemporary European intellectual movements is, to my
mind, Alex Callinicos's *Is There a Future for Marxism?* (London: Macmillan, 1982); Callinicos covers some of the same
ground in *Marxism and Philosophy* (Oxford: Oxford University
Press, 1983).

Since my own introduction to Jameson is quite literally
meant to be read alongside *The Political Unconscious*, I have
not footnoted the various sources (including Jameson's previ-

ous writings) on which its argument draws. To these, the readiest guide is Jameson's index and notes in *The Political Unconscious* (Ithaca, N.Y.: Cornell University Press, 1981).

Diacritics, vol. 12 (Fall, 1982), is a special issue devoted to *The Political Unconscious*. The issue contains useful commentary on Jameson's theory by, among others, Hayden White and Terry Eagleton, as well as an informative interview with Jameson.

Index

INDEX

Printed in Great Britain
by Amazon

24817208R00084